MICHAEL JACKSON
THE HOTTEST STAR
OF THE DECADE!

His music dazzles. His dancing electrifies. And his creative genius astonishes. Seven million fans turned *Off the Wall* into a platinum prize. The phenomenal *Thriller* album, which spawned the pace-setting Oscar-nominated video, broke the Guinness World Record with twenty-five million sold to date. And in 1984, he won an unprecedented eight Grammy's.

MICHAEL JACKSON: THRILL takes an intimate up-to-the-minute look at this megastar of the eighties—from child stardom with The Jackson Five to superstardom at twenty-five. Here's the real Michael Jackson and all the glitz, glamour, and flash that makes him today's most fabulous celebrity!

Michael Jackson Thrill

BY CAROLINE LATHAM

ZEBRA BOOKS
KENSINGTON PUBLISHING CORP.

ZEBRA BOOKS

are published by

Kensington Publishing Corp.
475 Park Avenue South
New York, N.Y. 10016

First printing: March 1984

Printed in the United States of America

Michael Jackson

Thrill

Contents

Introduction

**Michael Jackson steps out on the stage in Atlanta, in front of more than 50,000 screaming fans, nearly all of whom want to reach out and touch him. The thin wiry body struts, crouches, sways with the intensity of the lyrics — even stretches out flat on the floor before writhing to the insistent beat. The long legs flash and cut through the air, and the high exuberant voice never misses a note. The fans are on their feet, and the current of electricity flowing between Michael and the audience is practically visible. You know they won't sit down until he lets them.

**Michael Jackson sits alone in his room all

day Sunday. He is fasting, subsisting the entire day on nothing but liquids, in his own personal rite of purification. He reads, he daydreams, he talks on the phone to friends like Kristy McNichol and Diana Ross, he tries out a few dance steps, he chats with his mother or some of his brothers and sisters. It's a quiet day of contemplation, a period of total isolation from the world of showbiz glitter. It closes with Michael's prayers. It's certainly a far cry from the stereotype of the glamour life of the Superstar, but it's a routine Michael follows week after week.

**Michael works in the recording studio on one of the cuts for his long-awaited album, *Thriller*. He shows himself to be a tireless perfectionist, who drives himself and those around him to do the very best that is possible. He sings a few lines, stops the tape because he is dissatisfied. He does the phrase over and over, makes notes for the engineer about the way it should be mixed. Producer Quincy Jones tells him it's fine, but Michael is looking for something more, something better—he'll know it when he hears it. At last he gets it right, the song moves on to its conclusion. Michael throws up his hands in glee, shouts out his relief . . . and promptly starts a food fight, right there in the expensive high-tech state-of-the-art recording studio.

**Michael agrees to make an appearance at

the telecast of the American Music Awards (at which he will win an unprecedented eight awards). His friend Brooke Shields reads about it in one paper and calls to congratulate him. He casually asks if she'd like to be his date for the event. She leaves her dormitory room at Princeton (covered with Michael Jackson posters) and flies 3000 miles to California for just one evening. They are photographed holding hands, and the inevitable gossip begins. But a spokesman for Michael (sports promoter Don King) says firmly, "Love? No, I don't think it's that. They just like each other very much." And Brooke's mother says enigmatically, "Brooke loves him for what he is: the consummate professional."

**Michael hangs out with his brothers, still among those closest to him. They go out in the backyard of the house where he lives with his mother (a two-million-dollar mansion in Encino) and play a little one on one, they look at the animals in Michael's menagerie, they check on the construction of the Disney ride Michael has ordered installed for his personal pleasure. Watching them, they seem like any ordinary family, laughing and joking, shouting insults at one another, talking about their kids and their work. Until you begin to think about the extraordinary expensiveness of their toys. And the fact that there are bodyguards and guard dogs discreetly in evidence.

**Michael Jackson finally comes up with the concept for the video to promote the title cut from his new album, "Thriller." This light-hearted dash through a Chamber of Horrors becomes (thanks to Michael's fame and financial leverage) a big-budget production rumored to have cost more than a million dollars, with 20 make-up artists, 18 professional dancers, and hot director John Landis (*Animal House* and *Trading Places*) at the helm. And while the video was in production, Michael Jackson Productions was filming an hour-long documentary called *The Making of "Thriller."* Most artists give these videos away to promote their albums. Michael Jackson becomes the first to *sell* his video to MTV, and then on top of that, he sells the documentary both to cable-TV and to a videocassette manufacturer. The entire music world is stunned by the commercial shrewdness of these moves.

**Michael Jackson is, by accident, at home alone except for a reporter: family, bodyguards, the people who ordinarily protect Michael from the world by chance all happen to be away at the same time, leaving Michael on his own for a few minutes. The doorbell rings, and shy Michael is thrown into a panic. He lifts the curtain to peer outside; his voice is trembling. Finally, he forces himself to open the door—to find a perfectly innocuous messenger sent over with some sheet music he wanted. He smiles thankfully and goes back inside. You get the feeling that this sort of accident is *never* going to be allowed to happen again.

These vignettes suggest something of the complexity of Michael Jackson, both as a public star and as a private person. He is, in fact, something of an enigma to even his most devoted fans. For example, nearly everyone who meets Michael personally is struck by his quality of otherworldliness, his childlike innocence in the face of such "adult" motives as greed, envy, and pride. On the other hand, they are equally impressed by his thorough-going professionalism. He is devoted to his work — more than that, he is *dedicated*. Although at this stage of his career, his name alone would sell anything he put on record, he labors long and hard to make sure each of his recordings lives up to his high standards. There is nothing childlike or casual about Michael's professional behavior.

Another apparent paradox is the difference between the shy private Michael Jackson and the effervescent public figure. He surrounds himself with a protective wall of friends and family because it is genuinely difficult for him to deal with strangers. He spends most of his free time at home, and avoids situations where he will be thrown in with new people. Yet when he gets on the stage, or in the public eye, he appears to enjoy the limelight. He preens and struts, he makes emotional contact with his fans, he thrives on the rapport that he develops with millions of people. And even though he is continually dogged by reporters and photographers, he never acts petulant or sulky about their perennial presence. He smiles for the camera, he signs autographs, he behaves graciously. Even after the recent unfortunate accident when his hair caught on fire and the back of his head was badly burned, Michael smiled and waved at the crowd as he was carried on a stretcher to the waiting ambulance.

With Michael Jackson, even the subject of sexuality seems somewhat ambiguous. He speaks of his intentions of getting married and having a family. In one interview he hinted that he would like to marry Diana Ross; in another, he cautioned the reporter not to discount Tatum O'Neil as a possible Mrs. Jackson. On the other hand, there are persistent rumors that Michael Jackson is gay, and some of his publicity photos seem to be purposely androgynous, showing Michael with wispy curls on his forehead and a big diamond-and-pearl brooch. Yet despite the ambiguity, Michael remains a true sex symbol, capable of driving fans of either sex into a virtual frenzy of passion.

The one point about which there is neither ambiguity nor enigma is Michael's talent. Even as a 10-year-old child, he amazed audiences and critics alike with his vocal sureness and his imaginative dancing steps. As the years have gone by, the evidence of his wide-ranging talent has continued to mount. As a singer, he has demonstrated great technical proficiency in his control of his tenor voice, and his ability to blend in occasional falsetto notes with ease. The emotional power of his singing is equally masterful; he can make you cry in a tender ballad, make you echo his infectious high spirits when he belts out a dance number, make you uneasily aware of the darker side of human nature in his more recent story-songs.

He has also proved that he can write hit songs himself. Although he has never felt compelled to create all of his own material, the fact of the matter is that some of his greatest hits, such as "Beat It" and "Billie Jean," have been with songs he wrote himself. As a lyricist, he is allusive, poetic, sometimes vague, but always remembering to tell a story. As a composer, he has a sure feel for rhythm, a structural neatness, and an ear for unexpected harmonies.

And his talents continue to expand. It is obvious, on the basis of his performance in *The Wiz* and his current crop of videos, that he is a talented actor; and it's surely only a matter of time until he stars in a hit movie. He may well have a talent for working on the other end of the camera as well. Several critics have pointed out that in his videos, Michael Jackson has acted as the true artist in creating the visual images and their impact, and that he really should be given some of the directorial credit. He is planning to produce albums for other musicians in the near future — a logical next step for one who has thoroughly mastered the arcane mysteries of the recording studio. And, in his most recent major commitment, he has signed a contract with Doubleday to write his autobiography. It should be a fascinating document.

At 25, Michael Jackson stands at the top of his profession. Consider these facts:

His current album, *Thriller,* has sold nearly 5 million copies, making it the best-selling album in history.

He was nominated for 12 Grammy awardsin 1983, and walked off with 8 of the 12 — a record-breaker.

The videocassette of *The Making of "Thriller"* shipped an initial advance of more than 100,000 copies, the largest number ever for any production that was not originally a feature film.

Thriller has been a hot-selling album in 18 foreign countries, and Number One on the charts in 8 countries outside the U.S.

At the 1984 American Music Association Awards, Michael Jackson won awards in eight different categories.

Michael Jackson is the first recording artist in history to have seven tracks of a single album become top-ten singles.

Based on its summary of sales figures for 1983, *Billboard* acclaimed Michael Jackson the Number One recording artist of 1983.

In the highly competitive world of pop music, where stars can rise and fall in the space of a single year, Michael Jackson's achievement is awesome. He has been performing for more than 20 years. He had his first hit in 1969, when he sang "I Want You Back" with the Jackson Five, and his most recent in late 1983, with "PYT (Pretty Young Thing)" (from Thriller) hit the charts. He is a multimillionaire and probably always will be. His friends are a dazzling galaxy of the famous and talented: Katharine Hepburn, Jane Fonda, Liza Minnelli, Tatum and Brooke, John and Caroline Kennedy, Steven Spielberg, Paul McCartney, Diana Ross . . . the list goes on and on.

Michael Jackson's future can be anything he wants it to be.

Michael's comment on the subject of his future: "I want to continue to grow. To me, the biggest sin of all sins is to be given a gift, a talent, because it's actually a gift from God, to take that and not cultivate it and make it grow, that's the biggest sin in the world."

1

LITTLE MICHAEL ENTERS
SHOW BUSINESS

To understand how Michael Jackson became what he is today, you have to look back at his past. And although he is only 25, an age at which many stars are just being discovered, he already has a surprisingly long past in show business, with a career that stretches back more than 20 years.

Michael Jackson would be the first to tell you just how important his family was—and still is—to his career. The success of his solo career is firmly rooted in the Jackson family's musical foundations. In fact, by the time Michael was born, the Jacksons were already creating their own musical tradition.

Michael Jackson was born on August 19, 1958, the seventh of nine children in the family. His parents were Joe and Katherine Jackson, and they were a struggling working-class couple, doing their best to raise a family of lively and high-spirited children in the somewhat threatening environment of Gary, Indiana. A great many people moved to Gary in the late 1940s and early 50s, lured by the jobs at the steel mills and factories. But although it was in those days a good place to make money, it was not such a good place to raise a family. Only a short distance away from Chicago, Gary had become nicknamed "Sin City" because of the excessive amounts of drinking, gambling, and other questionable activities that went on there. For a family with six sons, the dangers of street life were very real.

But both Joe and Katherine Jackson were determined not to lose a son to the streets. They had worked too hard themselves staying out of the poverty that was the fate of most urban blacks to see their sons sink down again.

Joe had grown up back in Tennessee. He attributed his own stability to the rigorousness of his upbringing. "My father was very strict," he once commented. "He was a schoolteacher, and he treated me just like the rest of the kids in school. I'm glad that happened. I might not have been able to do the things I've done without a very strict raising." Joe would imitate that role model provided by his own father, and act as the stern disciplinarian to his children. His wife later explained, "Joe was pretty strict. I didn't have to be when he was."

Joe Jackson married Katherine Corse, a young woman from eastern Indiana, in 1949. As their family began to expand, they settled in Gary, living in a modest three-bedroom house (coincidentally, it was on Jackson Street). Joe had a steady job as a crane operator with U.S. Steel. When family responsibilities permitted, Katherine worked as a sales clerk at Sears. Money was tight, but somehow they managed.

Both Joe and Katherine were musical. Katherine once played the clarinet, and she liked to sing—especially old favorites like "Cotton Fields" and "You Are My Sunshine." Joe's interest had been more serious. He once admitted that he "always wanted to be in entertainment." Living just outside Chicago, he had the opportunity to hear the exciting new music that was emerging as the result of the migration northward of southern blacks to big cities that could support music clubs. It was the heyday of the Chicago blues, and of the hard-edged, blues-influenced bebop sound. Joe played guitar and sang with a Chicago-based group called The Falcons, formed in 1951. "We played mostly colleges and things . . . bars," he recollected. "It was a blues thing, which is what everybody was getting into." But The Falcons never moved beyond this limited world of one-night gigs. Joe concluded somewhat sadly, "We tried to be professional, but we couldn't get the right type of management, guidance, or contacts, so we never really did anything serious with it."

By the time Joe Jackson's own dream of success as an entertainer died, he had a growing family on his hands. The Jackson's first child, Maureen, was born in 1950. The first boy, Jackie (his real name is Sigmund Esco) came along a year later. Next was Toriano Adaryl, better known to his fans as Tito, in 1953. Jermaine was born the following year; in 1956, the next addition to the family was another girl, LaToya. Marlon came along the next year, and Michael the year after that, 1958. After a space of three years, Janet, the baby of the family, made the group complete.

Just taking care of this growing family was a full-time concern. There were the usual problems of health and safety. Jermaine came down with a serious kidney disease when he was only four, and for a while it was feared he might not survive. Tito broke his arm playing football; Marlon was hit by a car and suffered a skull fracture. There was also the problem of discipline, especially in a city where many young black kids were the victims of street violence. The activities of the young Jacksons were carefully monitored; they were forbidden to hang out on the streets or to stay out late.

Because the kids were at home a lot, they heard Joe Jackson and The Falcons practicing their numbers. Said Joe, "The boys would listen to the things we were trying to do, at rehearsals, and there were always instruments lying around. If you're around something a lot, you're gonna take part in it." Tito was the first to pick up an instrument; he began fooling around with his father's guitar. One day, his father came home and caught him at it. According to the family legend, Joe Jackson demanded to know what his son was doing with the guitar. Tito's answer was to play it for him. Tito himself describes the outcome. "One day, I remember my Dad walking in the door after work and he was carrying something behind his back. It was a guitar! A red one! Man, I was really excited. I'd been fooling with his, and I'd showed him I was serious about playing."

Soon the two older boys began to sing along with Tito as he played some of their current favorite songs from the radio—"My Girl" by the Temptations, Sam and Dave's "You Don't Know Like I Know," "Twist and Shout" by the Isley Brothers, and anything at all by James Brown. Their parents encouraged them to work at their music, because it seemed like a good way to keep them off the streets. Joe Jackson later said, "There wasn't much for the kids to do in Gary—except go to school and come back home. I had them play musical instruments and sing so they would be able to better their condition."

Vocally, the boys blended together beautifully right from the start. But the instrumental background was too thin. So Jermaine began to learn to play the bass, and they got two of the cousins to help fill in occasionally—Ronnie Rancifer on electric piano and Johnny Jackson on drums.

At first, the group consisted of just the three oldest boys, all of whom had turned into handsome teenagers. Then the next two, Marlon and Michael, wanted to join, and the group evolved to accommodate their talents. Both of the younger boys were excellent dancers, so they began to incorporate more choreography into their routines. The time was the mid-1960s, the period of Motown's dominance in the field of black pop music, and the Motown groups all used intricate dance steps as part of their acts. The Jackson kids started out by imitating such groups as The Temptations or Smoky Robinson and the Miracles. Michael also became fascinated by the way James Brown moved on the stage, and he learned to mimic him with uncanny accuracy.

As the kids got better and better, their parents began to take the possibilities of their talent more and more seriously. Katherine spent her evenings creating costumes for them to wear when they performed. Joe went to clubs in Chicago to see how other groups sang and moved; he always came back with new ideas to try out. He also began to spend money to buy instruments for the group. He later told a reporter from *Rolling Stone* wryly, "We went overboard. My wife and I would fight, because I invested in new instruments that cost so much. When a woman's a good mother and finds all the money going into instruments she doesn't like it."

But apparently Katherine Jackson accepted the fact that her sons' career was worth some investment. Already, as early as 1963, there were signs that it might pay off. That was the year when they won a talent show at the local high school, Roosevelt High. Later that year, they sang at a hospital over the Christmas season; one of Michael's early memories is being on the same program as Santa Claus.

When Michael first joined the group, at the tender age of four, his participation was limited to dancing some steps and playing the bongo. But gradually, his father and his older brothers realized that Michael had a natural affinity with the limelight. They agreed that he should become their lead singer. As oldest brother Jackie recalled, "He was so energetic that at five years old he was like a leader. We saw that. So we said, 'Hey, Michael, you be the lead guy.'

The audience ate it up. He was into those James Brown things at the time, you know. The speed was the thing. He would see somebody do something, and he could do it right away."

The following year, with Michael firmly established as the group's lead singer, The Jackson Five had their first paid engagement, an appearance at a bar in Gary, for which they were to be paid the princely sum of $8. But this modest job turned out to be more lucrative than they expected. "When we sang," Michael recently reminisced, "people would throw all this money on the floor—dollars, 10s, 20s, lots of change. I remember my pockets being so full of money that I couldn't keep my pants up. I'd wear a real tight belt. And I'd buy candy like crazy."

Soon the Jacksons were entering every local talent contest they could find. Says Michael, "Whenever there was a talent contest in Gary, we would all try out for it. At a very early age I learned that trying was very important—but winning was too. We didn't always win in the beginning, but after a time we started to pick up trophies. That was really an accomplishment because the competition was very real. Nearly everyone we knew was trying to get started in show business."

Throughout 1967 and 1968, the Jacksons gradually built a local reputation as a hot act. Not only did they continue to win talent competitions and earn money from their appearances at bars and nightclubs, but they even made a couple of singles for a local label. Steeltown Records was based in Gary and could get distribution only in the immediate vicinity. But they put out the first ever Jackson Five record (now an extremely valuable collectors' item). On the A side, they did "I'm a Big Boy Now," a straightforward rhythm-and-blues number that capitalized on the group's amazing youthfulness. The B side was a tune called "You've Changed." On both cuts Michael is singing lead, and his brothers provide either backup or response. The A side was a local hit, and was picked up for distribution by Atco, to be sold throughout the Midwest.

Somewhat later, the Jacksons made a second single for Steeltown. They did a song called "We Don't Have to Be Over 21 (To Fall in Love)" and backed it with "Jam Session," on which their father joins them briefly to play a little electric guitar. Neither of these songs had even the limited success of "I'm a Big Boy Now," and their father realized that such narrow regional exposure was not going to further their career. They would have to aim for the big time.

In those days, for black artists, that meant winning the talent competition at the Apollo Theatre in Harlem. In fact, even being invited to compete would be a boost. The Apollo's location in New York meant that people from major record labels would be in the audience, looking for hot new talent. All through the spring of 1968, Joe Jackson pushed his sons to get their act fine-tuned. He was satisfied with what he saw them do. He later bragged quietly, "It always looked good; the little ones on the side and the tall one [Jackie] in the center. And their voices blended well because of the family thing. There's a basic tone quality that's common to all of them."

Musician and record producer Freddie Perren later told a story about seeing the Jacksons that spring, when he was playing at a club in Chicago with Jerry Butler. "When I saw these little kids opening the show for us I really felt sorry for them and hoped the crowd would be kind to them. Michael was so little and innocent. You know how a crowd can be. Well, Michael just destroyed the audience. He was amazing, just an amazing performer. Hey, it was very rough trying to come on after that, let me tell you."

By this time, the Jackson kids were getting to be local celebrities. But their parents were careful to keep them firmly anchored to reality. They still had to do their homework every night, and they also had to practice and rehearse. Michael told a reporter from *Rolling Stone* that his father did not even try to make these rehearsals fun; even as children, they understood that what they were doing was work, serious business. The kids got very modest allowances. And they were expected to behave themselves. Katherine Jackson explained how she was able to exert strong disciplinary control of a family of nine children: "After you instill in the two oldest what they can and can't do, the others automatically follow."

But Joe Jackson tried to make sure that there was some balance in the boys' lives. He encouraged them to participate in active sports, took them to play sandlot baseball, taught them how to fish. Such activities gave them an outlet for their energy, and also gave the family a chance to spend time together. Said Joe, "A family has to be close. A father has to be close to his sons."

But somehow young Michael never really showed much enthusiasm for sports. He preferred to stay inside, to practice his dance steps over and over, to listen to other singers handling a difficult line and try to discover how they did it. "There was a big baseball park behind our house," he told *Newsweek*. "You could hear the cheers of the crowd. But I never had any desire to play baseball. I would be inside working, rehearsing." And his mother admits, "It was sort of frightening. He was so young. He didn't go out and play much. So if you want me to tell you the truth, I don't know where he got it [his performing ability].

29

He just *knew*."

In the summer of 1968, the Jacksons got their first chance at the big time, when they were invited to compete at the Apollo. Joe Jackson remembers that occasion well. "One thing about the Apollo Theatre, if you weren't good, you might get a few cans or bottles thrown at you. The kids were more afraid of that than anything else. We weren't afraid of losing the contest; we knew we had it. We just wanted the people to like us. They went out there and performed, and won. In fact, we got a standing ovation."

That win led quickly to the chance to perform in small theaters and nightclubs all over the country, as an opener for better-known black artists, such as the Emotions, Jackie Wilson, Gladys Knight and the Pips, even James Brown. For Michael, the chance to watch these headline acts in person was a wonderful learning opportunity. He always sat in the wings and viewed the entire performance with rapt attention. Over and over, he watched the dance steps, the moves with the microphone, the interaction with the audience. Then he would go home and practice these things himself.

At this early stage in his career, Michael's talent was primarily for skillful imitation. He could imitate James Brown so well that it was difficult to remember, watching him, that he was only a little boy in grade school. Once he saw or heard something that interested him, he was quick to dissect its components, learn them himself, and then perform the same movement or sound with composure and verve. This mimicry gave him a basic repertoire of moves and vocal mannerisms that were later to form the foundation for his own, more original performance ideas.

With Michael's performance as lead singer growing smoother every day, the Jackson Five were a hit with the audiences wherever they played. And not *just* with the audience either. Gladys Knight thought the kids were terrific and promised to tell her own record label about their potential. Bobby Taylor, the lead singer with a group called the Vancouvers, was also impressed. Don Cornelius, then a DJ in Chicago (later to have a hit TV show called *Soul Train*) thought they were phenomenal. Slowly, their names were beginning to be heard throughout the world of black pop music.

It was about this time that Joe Jackson realized that his sons had a serious chance at big national success. So he took a step that must have required great courage—and real belief in the Jackson Five. He quit his steady job as a crane operator, the job that had enabled him to support eleven people, to spend his entire time managing the career of the Jackson Five. From now on, the five young boys were to be the sole support of the family.

Once Joe stopped working at U.S. Steel, he

was able to take the boys to jobs much farther away from home. He borrowed a friend's Volkswagen bus and hit the road. They played theaters and nightclubs in Washington, in Philadelphia, in Kansas City, once even in Phoenix.

The traveling was hard, but it gave them the exposure they needed. And it gave them the chance to polish the act, to work enough to get all the moves down. When they finally did become a success, the Jackson Five may have been kids, but they were by no means amateurs.

The other thing Joe Jackson knew he had to do was make a deal for the Jackson Five with a major record label. He thought he might be in over his head, and so he looked around for someone to help provide them contacts and help with the negotiations. He finally found the man he was looking for in Richard Arons, a lawyer for the musician's union. For nearly a decade, Arons looked out for the financial and legal interests of the Jacksons.

But as it turned out the Jacksons didn't really need anyone with connections to get them a recording contract. Their own talent would open the doors.

Both Gladys Knight and Bobby Taylor, who had been impressed by the boy's performance, happened to record for Motown. They told the president, Berry Gordy, about the Jackson Five. He was interested in what he heard, but didn't make the effort to go hear the group himself.

Then it happened. In April, 1969, Richard Hatcher, the mayor of Gary and one of the first blacks in the nation to be elected to that office in a major city, realized that he needed to raise money for the coming campaign for re-election. He turned for help to his friend Berry Gordy; Berry agreed to send some of his Motown stars to do a benefit concert to help in the fund-raising drive. In fact, he generously offered one of his very top acts, Diana Ross and the Supremes. Hatcher in his turn decided to ask his other friend Joe Jackson if the Jackson Five, by this time real local celebrities, would also appear. Thus the stage was set for what Jackson Five publicists were later to refer to breathlessly as "Discovery Day."

Here is the Jacksons' official version of that momentous day. "The Jackson Five tore through songs, giving each one all they had. 'More!' 'Fantastic!' 'Great!' The crowd was jumping with enthusiasm. Pushing through the crowd to the foot of the stage completely unnoticed in all the excitement was Gary's mayor, and with him none other than Diana Ross! Diana was rocking back and forth, clapping her hands and saying 'Right on!' with the rest of the crowd. They mayor was smiling and moving in time to the music. 'See, Diana? These kids are great . . .' the mayor shouted above the J-5 sounds. But Diana didn't need to be told; she was sold!

"When their numbers were over, the Jackson Five smiled at the applause, waved, and ran right for the bus. They were shy but happy about their performance. 'Let's go; let's get out of here!' they said to their dad. Before they could pull away from their parking spot, a voice called to them. 'Don't go, Mr. Jackson; don't go!' The Jackson family looked. Their mouths dropped open. Who should be calling and running toward the bus but the mayor and Diana Ross herself."

Years later, Michael admitted that the story of the Jackson Five's "discovery" by Diana Ross was greatly exaggerated for publicity purposes. Diana was by no means the first Motown figure to tell Berry Gordy about the talent of the Jackson Five; he had heard about them months before. But it *is* true that Diana Ross was enthusiastic about the group when she saw and heard them, and it's probably also true that her opinion carried great weight around Motown. And it is undeniable that after she saw them that fateful day in Gary, Indiana, things began to change very quickly for the Jackson Five.

2

THE MOTOWN CONNECTION

Diana Ross's excited phone call to Berry Gordy about the kids she had seen in Gary set in motion a long chain of events that would lead, in little more than six months, to the first hit record by the Jackson Five.

The first thing that happened was that Gordy issued an invitation: would the Jackson Five like to come to Detroit and entertain at a party he was giving at his mansion? It seems an unusual, and somewhat patronizing, way to hold an audition, but perhaps he realized that the Jackson Five needed a live audience to be at their best. He flew the boys and their father to Detroit—a nice change from the tiring routine of the long ride in the VW bus—and the Jacksons set up their instruments and sound equipment out by the pool house. All of the Jacksons remember being impressed with their first look at a real mansion: the big house, the huge back yard ("like a golf course," said Jackie), an indoor swimming pool, the impressive buffet for the guests . . .

The task before them was a particularly daunting one. The audience was not just any old group of rich socialites—not by a long shot. They were the chief executives of Motown and some of its biggest stars—the Motown "family." The Jacksons found themselves in the unenviable position of having to perform their imitative numbers in front of the very stars who made the songs a hit. It speaks volumes for both their professionalism and their motivation that they were able to do such a thing.

Let alone do it successfully.

But they pulled it off. Michael remembers, "We did our show and they loved it. They gave us a standing ovation. Berry Gordy came over, and Diana Ross came over at the end of the show and she kissed each one of us. She said she loved what she saw and wanted to be part of what we do."

In just a few weeks, the Jackson Five had a recording contract with Motown. Although the contract has never been made public, it's possible to deduce most of its terms, for the

Jacksons certainly didn't at that point in their careers have the leverage to negotiate anything beyond the standard boiler plate. The Jacksons got a royalty rate of 2.7 percent—low, but not unusual for a totally unknown group. Motown controlled all of the other subsidiary rights to the commercial exploitation of the group. Calendars, TV shows, licensing of merchandising rights: all belonged to Motown. Perhaps even more important in the long run was the fact that Motown had the right to make all the decisions about the Jackson Five's career. Motown would choose the material they would perform and record, decide when and where they should appear in public, set up and monitor their interviews with the press, select their costumes, hand pick their entourage. Berry Gordy intended to manage their career the same way he had managed the careers of other Motown artists—with an autocratic hand.

At about the time Motown signed the Jacksons, the company was making a switch, by moving its headquarters from Detroit, the motor city that gave the label its name, to Los Angeles, the capital of the music business. So it seemed obvious that the Jacksons too should make the move out to California. They were ready and willing. Michael still has a vivid memory of their arrival. "When we got there we went to Disneyland. It was freezing in Indiana . . . The sun, the swimming pools, a whole other image, a whole other life. It was magic."

One version of the legend has it that most of the Jackson family stayed with Berry Gordy at first, until they found a house of their own. An alternate version has them all staying with Diana Ross. The one fact common to both stories is that Michael Jackson did indeed stay with Diana Ross. She told a reporter at about that time, "Michael won me over the first moment I saw him. I saw so much of myself as a child in Michael. He was performing all the time. That's the way I was. He could be my son." Later, she put more emphasis on Michael's admiration of her than vice versa. "There was an identification between Michael and I. I was older, he kind of idolized me, and he wanted to sing like me."

No doubt the attraction was mutual, and perhaps they did instantly recognize the ways in which they were alike. As Michael got older, these similarities seemed to increase. His voice sounded more and more like hers; his music began to cross over established boundaries the ways hers did; he became not just a singer but an entertainer, just as she was; they even began to look rather alike. And they have remained very close, through all the changes. They now can boast of a fifteen-year friendship — and in fickle Tinsel Town, that is a real rarity.

Whatever Diana Ross may have contributed to Michael's education about the demanding business of being a star, it seems clear that Motown considered itself chiefly responsible for preparing Michael, and the other Jacksons as well, for the demands of success. Motown expected the Jackson Five to be stars, and they acted accordingly. They taught the boys how to handle big audiences, how to deal with the press, how to respond to fans: in short, how to live in the limelight. Although the boys were already skilled performers, Motown hired professional dancers to help them work out their steps, and other professionals to help them work out their on-stage "ad libs," the little bits of business that seemed spontaneous to the audiences but were in fact very carefully rehearsed.

By late 1969, the Jacksons were ready. All they needed was the right song. Berry Gordy found it for them within Motown, from the songwriting team that went by the name "The Corporation" and actually included several talented songwriters and record producers: Gordy himself (he started out in the business as a songwriter), Freddie Perren (who later went on to write "I Will Survive" for Gloria Gaynor and "Reunited" for Peaches and Herb), Deke Richards, and Fonce Mizell. The song was "I Want You Back."

"I Want You Back" was actually a straightforward soul tune; in fact the writers originally intended it for Gladys Knight. But it was adapted for the Jacksons by altering the lyrics to capitalize on the astonishing youth of the group. The strengths of the song are Michael's get-down delivery on lead, and Jermaine's hot and fast bass line. Instrumentally, the rest of the music is somewhat muddy, and the back-up singing by the rest of the Jacksons consisted of little more than "ooh, ooh, ooh." When you listen to this song today, it seems evident that it is Michael who is really carrying it. Writer/producer Freddie Perren remembers how hard Michael worked at that studio session. "I would have him do the song and by the time we got to the end, it sounded so good, he had improved the performance so much, that I would have him go back to the beginning. This would go on. First the beginning was better. Then he'd keep on and the ending was better than the beginning. With every take he got better."

"I Want You Back" (backed with "Who's Loving You?") was released at the end of 1969. Within a matter of weeks, it had sailed to the top of the charts. Eventually, the single sold nearly four million copies. It was a stunning success.

And it spurred Motown into a frenzy of activity to exploit the group's success while they were hot. Their first step was to collect some Motown standards for the Jacksons to perform and have them cut an album. It was released within a few weeks of the single, and it too was a hit. It was called *Diana Ross Presents the Jackson Five*. The title suggests that Motown didn't yet realize what a monster hit they had on their hands, since they felt the need to bolster the album's sale by dragging in the name of Diana Ross. *Rolling Stone*'s reviewer deftly pricked that promotional balloon at the conclusion of his review: "Given any kind of decent material at all, the Jackson Five should be able to give us many years of good tight music. Who's this 'Diana Ross' anyway?" The album made the Top Five despite the fact that so many of the songs were just filler, covers of hits by other Motown groups, such as "Standing in the Shadow of Love," "My Cherie Amour," and "Zip a Dee Doo Dah."

Before the fans could forget the Jackson Five and that cute little Michael who sang the lead, Motown released another single, called "ABC." It repeated the formula that had worked so well for the first single—a rapid and driving bass line underneath a shrill but dynamic vocal by Michael in that soprano voice that was somehow surprisingly convincing when it talked about love. "ABC," also written by "The Corporation," was another hit. It rose to Number One on the charts, sold over two million copies, and won a Grammy for Best Pop Song of 1970. The Jacksons' third single, "The Love You Save," repeated the success of the first two, selling several million copies and hitting the coveted Number One spot on the charts.

By this time, it was the summer of 1970, and the Jackson Five were *everywhere*. They appeared on Ed Sullivan's television show (Michael still has a tape of that performance and views it nostalgically every now and again). They were also on *American Bandstand,* and *The Andy Williams Show.* And they had made a couple of live appearances: one in Philadelphia's Convention Hall and another at the Cow Palace in San Francisco. They had been featured in *Time* and *Life* and *Look*, as well as *Ebony* and *Jet* and *Black Star.* The family home, a comfortable house in the Hollywood Hills section, was already on the tour maps of celebrity addresses.

In just a few short months, life had changed forever for the Jackson family. Michael, as the youngest of the Jackson Five and also in a very real sense the star, was perhaps the family member who felt the change most acutely.

Did Michael Jackson ever have a chance to respond like an eleven-year-old kid to the simple happiness of his amazing success? Or was it too quickly buried in the grueling work schedule and the need to be protected from his fans? In certain respects, that first year of fame must have been something like a nightmare.

Consider just the work load alone. In their first year with Motown, the Jackson Five made four albums. That's a grand total of about 45 songs they had to learn, rehearse, and then record. Then there were the concerts, with their demands for costume fittings, choreography lessons, and plenty of rehearsals. The television appearances called for more rehearsals and more travel. And then there were the constant interviews of that first year, when all of America wanted to learn about each and every one of the Jackson boys. The work involved seems staggering—especially for a kid who still has to go to school and be in bed by 9:30 every night.

Then there were the problems of the fame. Teenyboppers stood outside the house, waiting for Michael and his brothers to emerge. Joe Jackson explained, "We have to have tight security. With stars like these, you never know when somebody out there is waiting to get their hands on one of them." They stayed in public school exactly a week before they transferred to a private school. But even there, protection of such celebrities was difficult. The principal got frequent calls from eager fans, and they were lined up outside the entrance with their autograph books every evening. In their live performances, the threatening aspects of such mass devotion were palpable. Critic Albert Goldman reported: "There is an explosion of adolescent chemistry that rivals the first teen bombs detonated by the Beatles. Sheets of screams hang in the air, hysterically contorted mouths and hands rise to the lights, scrimmages clog the aisles—the air of the *corrida,* the cockfight, the gladiatorial combat fills the plastic vastness."

When you're just eleven, no matter how cool you are, how self-possessed, how experienced in being a celebrity in Gary, Indiana, the whole thing must be a little frightening. Years later Michael told a reporter, "Being mobbed *hurts.* You feel like you're spaghetti among thousands of hands. They're just ripping you and pulling your hair. And you feel that any moment you're gonna just break." His mother added with concern, "Every time I'd go to a concert, I'd worry, because sometimes the girls would get on stage and I'd have to watch them tearing at Michael. He was so small, and they were so big."

One other change for the Jacksons was the fact that people outside the family were now making most of the decisions about their present as well as their future. A Motown exec told the press, "We provide total guidance. We provide their material, set their basic sound, and work out the choreographic routines." Joe Jackson, once the principal decision maker in all these areas, was reduced to lesser responsibilities. He told Ben Fong-Torres, "My role is getting the boys out of the studio." Then he added defensively, "I'm the legal guardian. They listen to me 100 percent."

It was no doubt true that the boys continued to listen to their father, but suddenly they had a lot of other people to listen to also. By the summer of 1970, their entourage was sizable. First, there was Suzanne de Passe, a young executive of Motown, whose real job was to see that the Jacksons did things the Motown way. Then there was Tony Jones, their road manager, who coordinated the logistics of their travel and appearances. They needed a chauffeur by now, since they were only secure after they had been whisked away in the big limo with the opaque windows. They also had a bodyguard, to help ensure their safety. And since they had finally given up the attempt to attend any sort of school, the entourage also included a teacher, Mrs. Rose Fine, to see that their educations didn't suffer because of their stardom. They even had a guard dog, a German Shepherd named Hobo (a writer for *Time* joked that he was "trained to eat anything, black or white, that's squeaky and carries an autograph book.")

And on any given day, there were usually other people around the Jacksons as well: a Motown photographer taking pictures that could be used for publicity purposes, a reporter from some magazine or newspaper who was getting a chance at a live interview, a publicist to act as chaperone and keep the reporters away from potentially dangerous topics such as drugs and politics, and assorted hangers-on of every kind. No wonder Michael began to cultivate the habit of staying in his room!

Actually, even though the Jackson Five were one of the hottest groups of the year, Michael still didn't have his own bedroom. The family decided to move from their house in Hollywood Hills; it was too accessible to their fans, and too close to the neighbors, who complained about the noise of Jermaine's bass and Johnny Jackson's drums. So they bought a house in the more remote San Fernando Valley, in Encino. The house was virtually a mansion itself, with a swimming pool, a badminton court, a basketball half-court, and an archery range. Located on the grounds there was a separate guesthouse, servant's quarters, and a playhouse; soon they were to add a small recording studio. But even though the house was sizable, and had such features as a sunken recreation room, it had only six bedrooms — for a family of eleven people. So Michael, Marlon, and Randy, the three youngest brothers, all shared the same room. The fact that even today Michael doesn't really like to be completely alone may stem from the fact that it was not a habit he was ever able to cultivate in his youth.

By the end of the summer, Motown had released the Jackson Five's second album. Titled *ABC*, it contained the hit single of the same name, and also their next hit, "The Love

You Save." *ABC* quickly made it into the Top Five on the charts. Amusingly, critics wrote about the album as if they were reviewing the output of long-established stars. For example, Arnold Brodsky in *Rolling Stone* pontificated, "A good Jackson Five song is one that is not only fast with heavily accented rhythm, but also loose and playful, with built-in irregularities and breathing spaces that Michael and the others can fill with their delightful vocal improvisations." In less than a year, there was apparently already an established set of rules for evaluating a Jackson song!

The next hit single was "I'll Be There," and it was also featured on the next album, somewhat unimaginatively entitled *Third Album*. Before the end of the year, they had cut one more album, *Christmas Album*. *Third Album* was the third Jackson Five album to hit the Top Five, but *Christmas Album* was less successful— perhaps because it was so obviously a Motown attempt to exploit the holiday season and the Jacksons' popularity.

The Jacksons closed out the year of 1970 by appearing before 50,000 fans in Madison Square Garden in November—a sell-out crowd. Not only the fans were thrilled; so were the critics. Vince Aletti called the performance "astonishing." He continued, "First of all, visually; the five brothers are beautiful, or perhaps only cute, but they have complete

47

control. There's none of the embarrassment of child stars, but the stunning assurance of young men. When Michael punctuated his rendition of "Who's Loving You?" with a graduated series of forward crotch-thrusts—a standard R&B crowd-pleasing gesture—one was struck not so much by his precocity as his perfection, his professionalism . . ."

By 1971, the Jacksons had settled into their new existence. Parents Joe and Katherine did all they could to keep the kids from becoming unbalanced by their sudden success. Joe Jackson told *Life* magazine, "They go to school, do their chores, play ball. They have to maintain their personal lives, because if an entertainer doesn't, that's when he can get the big head. I have tried to teach them to associate with everybody—it doesn't matter what class. Because all people are the same. The only differences is maybe some got a lucky break."

Everyone who came into direct contact with the Jackson Five agreed that they were truly nice kids: polite, well-behaved, deeply professional. In fact, one observer commented, "If anything, you sometimes thought they were too nice, that they didn't have enough freedom." The evidence suggests that some of the older Jacksons would have agreed with this analysis. Jackie and Tito were particularly conscious of the price they were paying for fame in the loss of personal freedom. Jackie told a reporter resignedly, "It's necessary for it to be this way, but I don't like the private life." He added— could it possibly have been sarcastic?—"Being good is part of the business." Not only were they separated from their peers by the aura of their celebrity, they also gave up most of their childhood to hard work. Tito told an interviewer that he found the work in the studio taxing: "Repeating songs over and over—that's a drag, man. It's hard." Jackie concluded rather grimly, "It's my job. My work is entertaining people."

Perhaps it is not surprising that the older brothers got married as soon as they were old enough to take such a step, quickly establishing their own households with themselves at the head; it must have been a welcome change from the heavily regimented days of their early success. Tito married in 1972 and became a father in 1973. That same year, Jermaine married Hazel Gordy, the daughter of Motown's head, in a lavish wedding at the Beverly Hills Hotel for 600 guests at a cost estimated to be more than $60,000. Jackie was the next to marry, in 1974. Only Marlon and Michael were left at home and Marlon was already looking around for a place of his own.

Unlike his brothers, Michael seemed content to have things remain as they were. When, several years later, younger brother Randy moved to his own apartment, Michael expressed wonder, commenting, "If I lived alone, I think I would die." He continued to be very close to his mother, and the fact that, like her, he had become a Jehovah's Witness, gave them a special bond. But his choice of staying in the protected world of home was based on more complex elements than simply his desire to stay close to his mother. The truth is that he was not really comfortable in that outside world that his older brothers wanted to rejoin.

People who knew the Jacksons noticed the difference. When the older boys wanted to go out and play basketball with friends their own age, Michael preferred to sit inside and listen to music or talk to adults. When they went to one of the parties at which Motown commanded their appearance, the older boys mingled while Michael sat alone and took notes in a little book or drew pictures—deliberately distancing himself as an observer rather than a participant.

With his family, he could laugh and joke. They teased him, the way older brothers will do, called him "liver lips," made him carry the baggage, threatened to beat him up if he got out of line. The relationships in his family were casual and relaxed. And on stage, he also felt comfortable. He was a thorough-going professional: he *knew* what he was supposed to do when he got up in the spotlight, and he never failed to do it. But when he was just Michael, in a room full of strangers, then he felt awkward, ill at ease. His solution was to stay away from such situations; and as is usually the case, the decision only served to make him less and less practiced, and therefore more and more uncomfortable. Home was the cocoon that kept him safe from such stressful encounters. So it's no wonder that he chose to stay there.

Except, of course, for the times that he emerged to appear as the lead singer of the Jackson Five. The Jacksons were still popular as ever with their first and most loyal group of fans, the teenyboppers. In the early 1970s, heated debates were carried on throughout grade schools and junior highs all across the country about which one of the Jacksons was the cutest, the handsomest, the best dancer, the coolest, the best musician, the one whom you'd really really rather marry. Loyalties were intense, and the fan mail for all the boys was enormous.

But although Motown had initially labelled the music of the Jackson Five "bubblegum soul," the execs began to perceive that the Jacksons were capable of reaching an even wider (and older) audience. Slowly, a strategy evolved for slipping the Jacksons into the cultural mainstream.

One of the first steps was the creation of a Saturday morning cartoon show based on the Jackson Five, and produced by Motown's own production company. The cartoon kids looked like the Jacksons and spoke like the Jacksons, thanks to excellent mimicry by the actors reading the parts. But the Jacksons' only direct connection with the show was that their music was played on the soundtrack.

Another early effort to establish a national audience old enough to count demographically came with the production of a television special called "Going Back to Indiana." It started with a song of the same name, then built into Jackson Five Day, in Gary, Indiana, on December 31 1971. Mayor Hatcher received them at City Hall and gave them the keys to the city, saying, "I'm proud today that the Jackson Five have carried the name of Gary throughout the country, and the world, and made it a name to be proud of . . ." Then they gave a concert at the high school, and ended the day with a big family gathering at the home of an aunt, complete with fried chicken and sweet potato pie, and dozens of cute little cousins. All of these goings-on were filmed, and they formed the heart of the television special. Guest stars included Tom Smothers, Bill Cosby, Bill Russell, and Rosey Grier. The ratings were really quite respectable. As soon as the show was aired, the Jacksons kicked off a grueling 50-city tour that took them from New York to Hawaii.

By 1972, the tours were world-wide; the Jackson Five had become an international success. They appeared in Japan, England, West Africa. Audiences loved these cute little American black kids, and everywhere they went, their performances were sold out. The Jacksons in their turn seem to have been somewhat bemused by their whirlwind introduction to these foreign countries. They said it was "funny" to watch their cartoon in Japanese. They labelled Australia "old-fashioned" because of the scarcity of color TV sets there. An English paper laughed about the fact that Michael told their reporter he was glad to be in England because he was interested in Bonaparte . . . but then nobody really expected him to be an authority on world history. Perhaps the real reason that the tour seemed to make so little impression on the Jacksons is that for them it was just another round of concert halls, no different from all the others.

By this time, the Jackson Five looked and acted like old veterans of show biz. In fact, some critics were beginning to complain that they were *too* smooth, too polished, too carefully choreographed. The one thing that their performances, both in person and on record seemed to lack was spontaneity. The blame for this probably lay in the circumstances of their rise to fame, as well as in the personalities of their mentors.

Since they became famous when they were still children it was no doubt considered safer for all concerned to have them meticulously prepared and rehearsed, to leave nothing to the whims of a group of young boys. Moreover, Motown was well-known to be a control-oriented label, that told all of its artists—even the grownups—what to perform and how and when to do it. In a sense the Jacksons were the ideal Motown group, since their youth provided a rationale for the autocratic tendencies of the company's executives. When Motown signed stars who already had established styles of their own such as Billy Eckstine and Sammy Davis, Jr., the results were disastrous. Motown was a well-oiled machine that broke down when faced with individuality.

And last, but by no means least, the influence of Joe Jackson also mitigated spontaneity. He was of a time and a generation that had learned the key to climbing out of poverty was hard work and good behavior. And despite the enormous success of the boys he had so carefully nurtured, he still worried about the need to keep them safe and secure in a threatening world. He had taken one great risk when he quit his steady job to gamble the whole family's future on the boys' success, and he was not disposed to take any more. The idea that you could get up on a stage and just "be yourself," say anything that came into your head, play any tune you were in the mood to hear, was one he would have rejected immediately.

No, as long as Joe Jackson and Motown had anything to say about it, the Jackson Five would do things according to the carefully worked-out formula that had served them so well already. That premise is obvious as you listen to the records they made between 1971 and the end of 1973. There were more hit singles: "I'll Be There," "Never Can Say Goodbye," "Mamma Pearl." There were more albums (although none of them quite as successful as those first three), such as *Maybe Tomorrow, Jackson Five Greatest Hits,* and *Lookin' Through the Windows.* But even though individual cuts sometimes came to life, the net effect was a little stale. The Jacksons' competitors—most notably those cute kids from Utah called the Osmonds—were gaining on them.

Moreover, as Michael's birthdays mounted up, he was no longer so cute and little. His face lost its babyish roundness and began to lengthen. So did his legs. Thus he no longer seemed like a diminutive phenomenon, but more like an ordinary teenager. It used to be funny to listen to that baby-faced boy get up and strut his stuff like James Brown, sing songs full of sexual innuendo that he seemed too young to understand (although not too young to put over to the audience). But as Michael became more obviously adolescent, the amusement faded. Something new was needed if the Jacksons were to survive.

Motown tried the idea of solo careers for the brothers, preparing a fall-back position in case the group lost its fans. Michael made the first solo album, *Got To Be There,* in 1972. Jermaine cut *Jermaine* and *Come Into My Life* in 1973. Jackie made *Jackie Jackson* that same year.

But what saved the Jackson Five from being stuck to their bubblegum music was the new sound of disco. Motown put producer Hal Davis to work with the Five, and at the end of 1973, they released the album *Get It Together.* Reviewer Vince Aletti enthused, "This is not only the Jackson Five's best album to date, but the most exciting album to come out of Motown this year . . . It's hard bumping music, produced to death, dense with electronics and gimmicky as hell, but producer Hal Davis has calculated his effect so perfectly that every overwrought minute works." Fans thought so too, and the Jackson Five's career got a shot in the arm.

They followed that up the next year with an even better album, *Dancing Machine*, which contained the hit single of the same name. Suddenly, they had made the transition. No longer just a cute act calculated to appeal to prepubescent jumpers and screamers, they were acknowledged to be a mature musical group. Disco patrons in their twenties and thirties were buying Jackson Five albums and going to their concerts. Michael, a teenage stringbean, good-humoredly introduced himself to audiences saying, "I used to be little and cute. Now I'm big and cute." The fans ate it up. Even the fact that Michael's voice had changed from boy soprano to a high tenor (with mixed falsetto) was not the disaster that some people had predicted. As one of the brothers breezily told a reporter, "We just stepped down a key; and kept on truckin'."

Validation of the fact that they had finally reached a mature audience came in late 1974, when they were booked to play in Vegas. They worked up a new act, got sister LaToya to join them on vocals, and little brother Randy to pound away on the bongos. One of the highlights of their performance was a duet by Randy and Janet (eight years old) in which Janet came slinking out in a feather boa and sang an imitation of Mae West; it never failed to bring down the house.

After years of competing against the noise of screaming fans, Michael found the respectful hush of Vegas positively delightful. He said, "It's quiet there. Then you can really show what you can do." In fact, they all liked working in front of more sedate and mature audiences. Jackie told a reporter that the Jackson hoped to move into the category of entertainers like Frank Sinatra, Sammy Davis, Jr., and Wayne

Newton. He explained, "They put out one record a year and still go to Vegas and pack 'em in." They all seemed somewhat disappointed when, a few months later, they played Radio City Music Hall and found it nothing at all like Vegas.

So by the beginning of 1975, the Jackson Five had come of age. While the younger ones were still teen-age idols, the group as a whole had found a new audience and moved on to greater musical sophistication. As the success of *Dancing Machine* demonstrated, they could still move records out of the store and onto the charts. Their future looked brighter than ever.

But signs of a major change began to be noticeable. The truth of the matter is that the Jacksons were growing restless.

3

GOING INDEPENDENT

Many people in the music industry thought that the Jackson Five were a Motown creation. "They" said that it was Motown that discovered them, signed them to a recording contract, provided the material that they performed, choreographed their moves, and promoted them to the wide public they were reaching in early 1975. Motown execs were certainly quick to agree and take credit for all the success of the Jacksons. And many observers thought they were entitled to do so.

But the Jacksons disagreed. Joe Jackson later commented emphatically, "It was my wife and I who cultivated the boys and refined their talent.

Motown put the word out there and took a lot of credit, but it started with the family." And the performers themselves naturally asserted that they could do more than Motown ever gave them credit for.

The Jackson Five wanted more creative control over their own careers. They told Motown they wanted to write some of their own material; they even played tapes of their songs that they had cut in their own studio. But Motown was adamant. *They* were the ones who knew the secret formula for the Jacksons' success, and they weren't going to turn this multimillion-dollar enterprise over to a bunch of teenage kids. In essence, they told the Jacksons to quiet down and keep on doing what they were told.

Perhaps the issue of creative freedom alone would not have been enough to make the Jacksons leave Motown. But there were financial aspects of the situation as well. For one thing, Motown's five-year contract had given the Jacksons a low royalty rate on the sales of their records, now that they were established stars, they could certainly expect to do better. Moreover, some of Motown's standard practices drove up the costs of making a record to new heights — and all those costs were ultimately charged against the Jacksons' share of the income. Motown liked to exercise what it called "quality control" by doing many more takes of a song than necessary, and often recording many more songs than could possibly be used. This was a drain on the performers' time, and it was also a costly way to ensure quality (as opposed to more economical methods such as giving the group more rehearsal time, for example.) So the Jacksons and their advisors were well aware that the profits from their recording career were not as large as they might have been.

Another financial aspect of the Jacksons' lack of creative control lay in the way the money from the sale of a record is customarily divided up. A share—always small—goes to the artists who perform on the record. Then there's a share for the writers of the song. Another share goes to the publishing company that owns the rights to the song. And often another share goes to the production company that actually puts the master recording together. As things stood between the Jackson Five and Motown, the Jacksons got only the artists' share of the money from their recordings. Motown got all the rest. Its employees, disguised as "The Corporation," got the writers' share; its publishing company got the publisher's share; its production company got the production share. In fact, when other artists imitated the Jacksons and covered one of their hits, the Jacksons didn't make a penny from it—although Motown certainly did.

So more creative control would also mean more money, a share of the profits for writing and publishing and producing. Joe Jackson was anxious to see his sons reap those rewards. So sometime in the spring of 1975, a cautious search began for another record contract. The Motown deal would come to an end in March of 1976, and preliminary talks with Motown indicated that it would not meet the Jacksons' demands. The chances are good that Joe Jackson and lawyer Richard Arons talked to a number of labels, but the one they ended up deciding to sign with was Epic, a subsidiary of the powerful CBS communications conglomerate.

The new six-year contract was announced at a press conference in July of 1975. The Jacksons ;were tactful about their reasons for leaving Motown. They said that they had made the switch in the hope of selling more albums — it was generally conceded that Motown was oriented toward the singles market rather than the album-oriented audience — and of getting the kind of promotion that only a giant in the industry could offer. It *was* clear that they got a better deal from Epic, although just how much better, no one was saying. Joe Jackson said the contract was for "anywhere between $1 million and $30 million," a vague answer but one that meant that their rewards would of course be based on their performance. Joe Jackson told the press, "Everyone knows that the *business* side of the entertainment business is where the really big money is, and it is that side that I've always wanted the fellows to be deeply involved in. When they were with Motown, they were quite young and they had a contract that didn't permit them to do certain things. They did what they were told to do. Now they're no longer kids and they have a new contract with Epic which allows them to write their own material, they have their own publishing company, and they can produce their own albums. These are some of the key things I've always wanted for them."

No amount of tact was enough to soothe the wounded feelings of Motown. Execs were angry not only that the Jacksons were leaving but also that they had announced their departure nearly nine months before the contract expired. The relationship took an ugly turn, and Motown decided to sue for damages to recover the money they felt they had lost when it became public knowledge that the Jacksons were going to leave Motown. They had an album, *Moving Violation*, ready to release, and they contended that the album's sales had been hurt by the knowledge that the Jacksons had repudiated Motown. *Something* hurt the sales, because the album did not do well.

Motown established in court that they owned the rights to the name of the Jackson Five, and they blustered about planning to establish a new group under that name (using, they said, some of the thousands of musical Jacksons in the United States.) And eventually, they also established the fact that they had lost income because of the premature announcement, and the Jacksons had to pay damages of more than $600,000.

But presumably the Jacksons thought that cost was worth it. They were out from under the tight control of Motown, and ready to show what they could do on their own.

Or so they thought. But, to their surprise, Epic execs began telling them that they weren't yet "ready" to go out on their own. Epic would select a producer. The producer would pick the songs for their first Epic album and decide on the sound for The Jacksons, as the group was now called. It was a disappointing turn of events for the Jacksons. After all, if they wanted to be told what to do, they could simply have stayed with Motown.

But their professionalism triumphed over their disappointment, and they threw themselves into working on the Epic album, called *The Jacksons*. In actual fact, they were still five Jacksons in number, but a slightly different five. Randy had joined the group for good, as an equal partner. And Jermaine was gone. Obviously, since Berry Gordy was now his father-in-law, he had been placed in a very difficult position when the Jacksons left Motown. He later told a reporter, "It seemed that the whole world was against me. People didn't seem to realize that I had two families and that whatever I decided to do with my career wouldn't make me love either of them any less. I wasn't choosing between families. I was choosing between record companies." Apparently Motown bent over backward to keep him, considering it a kind of moral victory. They promised to do everything they could to promote his solo career. So he stayed with Motown—and his father-in-law. His own father was mad; his brothers were sad. Michael was wistfully, "Ever since we started singing, Jermaine was always in a certain spot near me on stage. All of a sudden he was gone. It felt bare on that side for a long time."

Jermaine's departure was the first major change within the group that had been so successful, and for a while there was speculation about whether the group could surmount the difficulty. Their new producers, however, took the whole thing in their stride.

Epic had matched up the Jacksons with veteran producers Kenny Gamble and Leon Huff. This pair had recently created what was called the "Philadelphia Sound" for groups like the O'Jays and the Blue Notes. The elements of this sound included a simple and repetitive tune, strongly in the mold of rhythm-and-blues, and a lush orchestration. The idea was to blend the Jacksons' straight-ahead Motown sound with the rich backgrounds of the Philadelphia sound to create music that would appeal to listeners of all ages. Although the Jacksons were chagrined at finding themselves once again singing someone else's songs under someone else's direction, they gave it their best shot. The result was an album called *The Jacksons,* released in late 1976. One cut from the album, "Enjoy Yourself," sold over a million copies, but the sales of the album itself were somewhat disappointing; it went gold (barely), but not platinum. And for the first time, a Jackson record got some very negative reviews. For example, *High Fidelity* called it "a considerable disappointment," and went on to say that "their funny exuberance doesn't blend easily into the slick Gamble and Huff production, and the great Michael Jackson has been reduced to just another voice." *Rolling Stone* observed that Gamble and Huff "channel the group into drab disco numbers and shabby ballads. The instrumentation, by various Jacksons and MFSB [a Gamble and Huff roup] is perfunctory."

Perhaps the Jacksons' only consolation at this moment was the fact that their anthology album, issued by Motown and comprising cuts of their greatest Motown hits, was doing very well. Their old fans were still loyal.

Epic hurried the Jacksons back into the studio with Gamble and Huff to cut an album that was intended to repair their reputations. But it simply repeated the same formula— apparently Epic believed in doing it over until you get it right. It was released in 1977 under the title *Goin' Places*. But that's just what the album failed to do. It was the first real bomb the Jacksons had ever put out, and not one cut had any success as a single.

Things must have looked rather bleak to the Jacksons at that point. Their move from Motown certainly hadn't made things any better. (On the other hand, Jermaine's decision to stay with Motown hadn't worked too well either. He had made two albums, *My Name is Jermaine* and *Feel the Fire*, and his solo career seemed to be going nowhere.) Although their concerts were still sell-outs, their record sales were declining. And they hadn't had a Number One single as a group since 1971, with "Mama's Pearl." What was wrong?

Cynics said they should never have left Motown (and no doubt Motown execs agreed). Motown "made" them, people said, almost as if Berry Gordy had whipped up Michael Jackson in his basement laboratory. Motown had "understood their limitations"—meaning, one supposes, that they were all too young to have any sense. Writers began comparing Michael with Frankie Lymon, another black child star, who sank into obscurity when his voice changed and finally died of his drug habit when he was only 26. Was Michael too on the way down?

But the Jacksons disregarded all the gossip and found their own cure for the problem. They marched into the offices of Epic and demanded a change for their next album. This time they wanted to be in charge. Epic execs had to admit that their own strategy of putting the Jacksons into the hands of strong and experienced producers hadn't worked out too well. So they agreed to take the gamble and let the Jacksons make an album *their* way. The Jacksons would write most of the songs. They would produce the record. They would even be consulted about record jacket design and promotional techniques.

The resulting album was prophetically called *Destiny*, and it put the Jacksons back on top. The album sold one and a half million copies. Two hit singles came out of it: "Shake Your Body (Down to the Ground)" and "Blame It On the Boogie." The Jacksons' own sound was looser, funkier than anything they had achieved under the tight control that had usually been their experience in the studio. Michael's vocals particularly benefited from the new freedom; he sounded more enthusiastic, more vital, than he had for years. His cheerfulness is totally infectious to the listener, and a large part of the reason for the album's success.

The Jacksons were naturally delighted to see *Destiny* sell so well, and to watch the singles move to the top of the charts. Michael expressed their feelings when he said, "I'm really proud to say that my brothers and I feel good knowing that we proved to ourselves and to others who doubted us that we could come up with a smash hit like the *Destiny* album."

Michael also commented that making *Destiny* had almost been like starting a career all over again. It certainly seemed to have the effect of rekindling their creativity and enthusiasm, both as a group and as individuals. They began to think about doing new things, accepting new challenges. As Michael put it, "All of us think we've got whatever's necessary to appeal to everybody. Plus, we're still young and there are all kinds of other things ahead of us — more writing and producing, movies, TV . . . all kinds of things. I think all the fellows would agree that right now we're all very happy people, we love what we're doing and what we're going to be doing and can't wait to bring it forth."

As the lead singer and star of the Jacksons, Michael of course was the member of the group who was offered the most opportunities for solo work. But the other brothers too were moving out to find projects on their own. Jackie, always the brother most interested in the business aspects of the Jacksons' career, began looking around for business opportunities. Tito was getting into producing other people's records. Randy, who shared co-writing credit with Michael on many of *Destiny*'s best songs, wanted to write his own songs, and perhaps hear them performed by other groups.

And of course, they had their personal lives to consider as well. Jackie, Tito, and Marlon were all married, and they were all fathers as well. Since they were raised in a close-knit family themselves, it is not surprising that they wanted to spend time with their own families. Heaven knows they had earned a bit of a vacation. By the end of 1978, the Jacksons had been working hard in the music business for more than a decade. They had made thirteen albums as a group, and nine more solo albums scattered about the family as well. They had toured the world, done a command performance for the Royal Family in England, played Vegas and Radio City Music Hall, filled large concert halls to capacity. They had been on the cartoon heroes of a Saturday morning program, guested on a number of variety shows, had their own special, and (in the summer of 1976) even had their own summer replacement variety show. That's a lot of hard work for a lot of years.

And of course by this point, all the Jacksons were financially secure so they could choose exactly when and how they would work in the future. All the money they had made as a group had been divided up into equal shares, and managed intelligently for them. When a reporter from *Ebony* pressed them to tell exactly how rich they really were, Michael answered snappily, "Talking about how rich you are and standing next to fancy cars and things is tacky and tired. Just say that we've been out there working a long time and we've been financially successful." In fact, all of the Jacksons are multimillionaires—and therefore never need to work another day in their lives.

Unless, of course, they want to. And they do. Three years after *Destiny*, Epic released another Jacksons album, called simply *Triumph*. And once again, the Jacksons were in complete creative control. The songs were written by Michael, Randy, and Jackie. The Jacksons produced the album themselves, and they were a bit freer about sharing the lead vocal tasks than ever before in the past. Not only Michael sings lead, but so do Randy, Marlon, and Jackie on certain cuts. *Triumph* was another platinum album for the Jacksons, and another critical success as well.

England's prestigious *Melody Maker*, which is capable of more cruelty in reviews than is ever seen in the United States, glowed, "The album doesn't have a weak track on it, and the Jackson writing, producing, and performing combines to make as strong, exciting and satisfying a pop record as we're likely to get before Christmas. Its title is no exaggeration." Davitt Sigerson, writing in the *Village Voice*, concentrated primarily on the writing skills of Michael Jackson. He said, "Once again, he is the ubiquitous voice of black popular music, but he can become something more. Already, with 'Shake Your Body,' 'Don't Stop 'Til You Get Enough,' and 'Lovely One,' he has written a new kind of hit single with rhythms derived so directly from his stammeringly erotic singing style . . . different enough to constitute the foundation of a genre."

Triumph contained three hit singles. There was "Lovely One," with its rich and unusual chords and Michael's driving vocal. Second was "Can You Feel It," which opens with a few bars and rich chorale sound, moves smoothly into the verse, and then breaks wide open for the chorus. "Heartbreak Hotel," written by Michael alone, is a strange and self-revealing song that is a precursor of his later hit, "Billie Jean." "Heartbreak Hotel" tells of the singer's haunting by the spectre of his former loves—all of whom seem to be in an accusatory mood. About this song, Sigerson wrote, "self-chastisement, paranoia, and adolescent morbidity are common in R&B; sexual delight and romantic loyalty are not. It is Jackson's lot to embrace both and to let them play, often perhaps out of control."

Throughout the late 1970s and early '80s, there were continual rumors that the Jacksons were "breaking up." Such gossip was based on the fact that Michael's solo career had by then become so successful, as well as on the fact that the other brothers were continuing to involve themselves with business activities on their own too. But the Jacksons always denied the rumors. Jackie said, "Right now we're each doing individual things. I'm more into producing and writing; so is Michael. He's making some movies. We've been doing that for quite a while now, but we're doing more of it right now. [This was in 1981.] But we're still going to come back and do concerts and things like that." Randy amplified, "The Jacksons will still produce and record their albums. But we're spreading out a little more giving ourselves a little more space to be more creative, to do more writing or singing or whatever we want to do — acting, producing, whatever. Sometimes it's more space to do other things that're needed and still sing together."

It was left to Michael to put the rumors to rest. He said conclusively, "My brothers and I get along fine. There's no ego problem with us; each of us knows what the other can do, and we think everybody has a role in our act. Right now we feel the Jacksons are still in evolution. It's just not the time to make any drastic change. I'll do more films and my own albums but right now the group comes first." He added cryptically, "Anyway, I don't do very many things until a certain force tells me to do them. The force tells me when and then I make my move."

It seems clear that the decision about keeping the Jacksons together is basically Michael's. Because he remains the star of the show. Of course, the other Jacksons have found things to do on their own. Randy continues to write his own songs and to work on a solo album. Marlon has his own production firm and is working with several other singers. Tito has produced an album for RCA. Jackie continues to work in various business enterprises. But none of the other brothers has had Michael's success. So, despite the creative contributions of Marlon, Tito, Jackie, and Randy, the Jacksons more and more seem to be Michael's backup group. As John Rockwell said of a recent concert appearance, "It was pretty much a Michael Jackson show, with musical and choreographic accompaniment by his brothers."

What's in it for Michael? Presumably, he likes the comfort of performing with his brothers. No artist can do a big concert appearance as a solo act; it's just too much strain. And what better backup group could Michael find than his own brothers, who have developed musically along with him for the past decade and half? Although performing with the

Jacksons is no longer the focal point of Michael's career, it's a good bet that he will continue to do it as long as the act is viable.

In the summer of 1981, the Jacksons made the biggest concert tour of their entire career. They appeared in 36 cities, and they grossed well over $5 million. The show itself was conceived by Michael, and it contained a number of different elements, such as video clips of their earlier performances (that appearance on the Ed Sullivan show is always a favorite with their fans) and even a magic act. They sang medleys of their old Motown hits, and then performed numbers from their Epic albums (as well as a few cuts from Michael's solo album). The tour was such a success that Epic decided to put out a double LP, called *The Jacksons Live*, based on live recordings of their concerts. (It was also a sly way to get some of their biggest Motown hits into the Epic catalog.) Despite the high price associated with a double album, *The Jacksons Live* sells well.

As of this writing, the Jacksons have not made another album together. They did appear together on the television special, *Twenty Years of Motown*, in a rare reunion that included Jermaine. (He has continued to record for Motown, and has now released a total of nine albums . . . none of which has done very well.) Their appearance was one of the highlights of a very special evening. And they have plans for another concert tour in the summer of 1984. It's sure to be a sellout wherever they go.

The Jacksons can look back on their 15-year career as recording stars with satisfaction. Michael points out, "I guess some people don't feel The Jacksons, a black group, can sell over 90 million records . . . They forget that good music is colorless." But on a more philosophical note, he reflects soberly on the luck that came along with the Jacksons' talent. "I've always thought of success and failure as being somewhat like two girls—one who's super beautiful, the other one quite unattractive. The beautiful girl, who could represent success, shouldn't be boastful about her beauty; she shouldn't go around bragging about it, and she shouldn't poke fun at the less attractive girl. Neither girl made herself; God made them both. I feel that way about the success the Jacksons have achieved. We didn't make ourselves; God did. And He gave us whatever talent we have, and we always think He's projecting something through us for the whole world to share and enjoy. That's how we have always seen ourselves."

4

MICHAEL AND THE MOVIES

In late 1978, Michael Jackson had an interview with a reporter from *Black Stars*. He began the proceedings by jumping up to put on the tape of the Jackson Five performing on the *Ed Sullivan Show*. "I often view this tape," he said. "I was eleven years old then, I believe. It seems so long ago—then it doesn't. I daydreamed about being an actor even in those days. I know that many people will never fulfill their dreams and wishes, and I'm very happy that I'm fulfilling one of mine."

The minute he stepped out on the stage, the young Michael Jackson was acting. He was acting the part of a grown-up rock star, even though he was only a ten-year-old boy. He was acting the part of James Brown, or Jackie Wilson, or the lead singer of the Temptations, mimicking their moves, imitating their projected passion. And he won the audience over every time.

So it is no wonder that he nursed the dream of acting in a movie. For years, there had been rumors that the Jacksons were going to star in a movie. They made it clear that they were interested, and it seemed an obvious step for Motown, since the corporation also owned a production company that made feature films (including *Lady Sings the Blues* and *Mahogany,* both starring Diana Ross). But no property turned up that was appropriate for one entire group; it would, after all, be an unusual script that had starring roles for five black teenagers.

But Michael still hoped that something would turn up—for him, if not for the whole group. And thanks to his friend Diana Ross, it did. Motown had come up with another vehicle for its favorite movie star, and bought the rights to the successful Broadway show, *The Wiz,* a black musical version of *The Wizard of Oz*. On the face of it, it seems an odd idea. The star of *The Wiz* on Broadway was diminutive Stephanie Mills, a talented teenager who looked even younger than she was. Diana Ross, on the other hand—well, it certainly *was* on the other hand. She was in her thirties, and her image was that of a sophisticated lady . . . not an easy fit with the character of Dorothy. In fact, to accommodate her age, the plot had to be changed so that the heroine Dorothy was no longer a young girl but a spinster school teacher, still living at home while her family tried to marry her off. This change created a dubious lead-in to a children's story of imaginative adventure, but Diana herself seemed to have no qualms.

Neither did a number of other talented people. Universal Studios became partners in the venture. Sidney Lumet, whose previous successes included *Dr. Stranglelove, The Pawnbroker, Serpico,* and *Murder on the Orient Express,* agreed to direct. Comedian Nipsey Russell would be the Tin Man, veteran Ted Ross would play the Cowardly Lion. Richard Pryor had a cameo role as the Wizard himself. And in an inspired piece of casting, Lena Horne was to be Glinda the Good. But who would take the role of the gangling Scarecrow? Diana thought of her friend Michael Jackson, who not only looked the part but had the necessary dancing ability too.

She probably had her work cut out for her selling the idea to the executives of Motown, since the time was just after the Jackson Five had left Motown and moved on to Epic. But whatever Motown may have felt about the Jacksons at that point, they had to admit that Michael was really perfect for the part of the

Scarecrow. As an added plus, the warm personal relationship between Michael and Diana could be expected to come across on the screen, in the scenes between Dorothy and the Scarecrow. So in the end, the part was Michael's.

He immediately began to study the script. He also looked carefully at the classic MGM version of *The Wizard of Oz*, with dancer Ray Bolger playing the part of the Scarecrow. Michael knew he was up against a challenge. He said, "I love my role but it takes studying, concentration, and faith that you will do the very best when the cameras start rolling." Part of what gave him that faith was the knowledge that he was working with a group of seasoned professionals. "There are so many supertalented people involved with *The Wiz*. I knew that I was working with the best folks so I had nothing to worry about."

But it seems that he *was* a little bit worried after all. Just before the movie started shooting, Michael's health seemed in danger — possibly from the work he had put into preparing for his role. He explained, "I had a lung attack on the beach on the Fourth of July. I couldn't breathe. They had to rush me to the emergency hospital. The doctor said it was pneumonophorax, bubbles on the lungs, and the bubbles burst and you can't breathe." Luckily, he was back on his feet by the time he was to begin shooting.

Michael believed that this movie version of *The Wiz* came closer than any other to capturing the essence of the original story by L. Frank Baum. "I think that the stage and the MGM version kind of missed the point. The message is that these people are looking for something they already have. It's inside of them already, but they don't know it because they don't have that belief in themselves to realize it. Lots of brilliant people are walking around today who never reach the higher ground because they don't have belief, and that's what L. Frank Baum is trying to get across through using these characters. It's like a fable. Like Aesop used animals. A lot of people may call it a kid story. But it's not."

Michael was grateful for the support he got from the other professionals connected with *The Wiz*. He said that Diana Ross remained "a good friend on the set and we sometimes held personal conversations for hours in between scenes. We even read the script together sometimes. From the first day of shooting, Diana has been telling me how wonderful I am and how proud she is of me; and the beautiful thing about it is she really means what she says." He was also full of praise for Sidney Lumet. "Sidney helps me in my character. He is a fantastic director. He wants to be sure I understand the role of the brainless scarecrow

. . . And I listen to the director to make sure I really understand. I learned from a previous experience—a TV special—I didn't understand anything at all that I was doing."

In his turn Michael showed himself to be as willing to work hard as ever. One of his most difficult tasks came in a scene where he was supposed to carry the unconscious Diana Ross. "She's heavy!" he complained jokingly. He did his best to gain weight so he could manage the feat. He endured the every-morning ritual of spending three hours in makeup and another hour getting into his elaborate costume, without any complaint. In fact, many people on the set noticed that Michael hated to take his makeup and costume off at night and occasionally he was allowed to go home (to a hotel room in New York) still dressed as the Scarecrow. He later explained, "When it's time to go off [the stage] I don't want to. I could stay up there forever. It's the same thing with making a movie. What's wonderful about a film is that you can become another person. I love to forget. And lots of time you totally forget. It's like automatic pilot. I mean—whew!"

Since Michael's face was virtually hidden behind his heavy scarecrow makeup, most of his acting had to be done with his body rather than his face. And as Michael played the Scarecrow, dancing was an integral part of that acting. He admitted to being inspired by Ray

Bolger's performance, but in many ways, his own characterization of the Scarecrow was more fully realized. Michael observed, "All scarecrows are wobbly. I am especially, because I just came off the pole so I can't walk." His descent from the pole, where we first see him, became one of the highlights of the film. He was funny, touching, seemingly on the brink of collapse but always somehow in graceful control of his movements. Within just a couple of minutes, and by movement alone — almost like a mime — Michael managed to convey the essence of the Scarecrow's character, and to establish him as the leading hero of the story to come. It was a bravura performance, especially for a film debut.

As a musical, *The Wiz* required not only dancing but also singing. Michael and Diana duetted the hit song of the Broadway show, which also became the hit song of the film and was finally released as a single, "Ease on Down the Road." It seemed logical also to give Michael a song of his own. There had been a song for the Scarecrow in the original Broadway score but it was cut before the show opened. Michael began to work on adapting that song for his voice, and his characterization of the Scarecrow. He worked in collaboration with the film's musical director, Quincy Jones.

Jones, who remembered seeing Michael sing the title song from *Ben* at the Academy Awards show five years earlier, was impressed by Michael's new maturity. He said, "I saw another side. Working with him in the context of being an actor, I saw a lot of things about him as a singer that rang a lot of bells. I saw a depth that was never apparent, and a commitment. I saw that Michael was growing up." It was during the time they worked together on *The Wiz* that they agreed that Quincy would produce Michael's next album—a decision that was to bring both of them great success in the future.

When *The Wiz* was finally released, the results were disappointing to most of the people who had worked on (and invested in) the film. The only list *The Wiz* ever made was the list of the most expensive films ever produced; it cost more than $24 million. But in a year that saw the release of *Grease, Close Encounters of the Third Kind,* and *Animal House, The Wiz* was a box-office flop that never recouped even as much as half the money invested in it. And aside from a nomination for the film's cinematographer, *The Wiz* was also totally ignored by the Academy Award voters. Even in the musical categories, such a Best Song and Best Score, *The Wiz* was pushed aside by *The Buddy Holly Story*.

And for the most part, critics were not kind. Most of their dissatisfaction was focused on Diana Ross, who probably did bite off more than she could chew in pitting herself against audiences' memories of the young and luminous Judy Garland. Diana simply seemed too old, too sophisticated to touch our hearts as Dorothy. Moreover, by making her a lonely and frustrated spinster and the trip to Oz an escapist fantasy, the ending of the film was undercut; there seemed to be no reason for Dorothy to go to so much trouble to return home. But even the most hostile reviews generally made an exception in the case of Michael Jackson. All agreed he was well cast, and made the Scarecrow an amusing and sympathetic character. And both his singing and his dancing were commended.

So whatever other people lost in making *The Wiz,* Michael Jackson came out a clear winner. Suddenly, he was in great demand for screen roles. At one point it was announced that he would star in a movie called *Summer Stock,* "about this boy and his pal trying to make it in show business in the chorus line," to be produced by Ken Harper, who was the executive producer of *The Wiz.* Later, there were stories about Michael's efforts to initiate a film that would tell the life story of famed black dancer Bill "Bojangles" Robinson. But as of this writing, no film project involving Michael Jackson has gotten past the announcement stage.

But he continues to be fascinated with the medium and to think about making another film. Through Quincy Jones, Michael was introduced to Steven Spielberg, and the two of them hit it off immediately. Quincy was doing the music for a record version of Spielberg's *E.T.,* and both men thought Michael would be the ideal candidate for narrating the story of the gentle visitor from outer space. Spielberg told Michael, "If E.T. didn't come to Elliott, he would have come to your house." Michael was devoted to the character of *E.T.* When he visited the set, Michael responded to the special-effects character as if it were alive: "He grabbed me, he put his arms around me. He was so real that I was talking to him. I kissed him before I left."

When Spielberg asked Michael if he would participate in the album project, Michael said yes immediately. He found working on the project to be a moving experience. He told an interviewer from *Ebony,* "When I was doing that recording, I really felt that I was E.T. and it was because his story is the story of my life in many ways." He amplified, "He's in a strange place and wants to be accepted—which is a situation that I've found myself in many times when traveling from city to city all over the world. He's most comfortable with children, and I have a great love for kids. He gives love, and wants love in return, which is me. And he has that super power which lets him lift off and fly away whenever he wants to get away from things on Earth, and I can identify with that." In fact Michael says he believes that human beings *can* fly. "We just don't know how to think the right thoughts and levitate our selves off the ground."

Speilberg was delighted with Michael's performance in telling the story of E.T. He commented, "Michael is one of the last living innocents who is in complete control of his life. I've never seen anyone like Michael. He's an emotional star child." The only trouble Spielberg had with Michael came when he was to narrate the part of the story where E.T. is dying. Michael sat in the darkened studio and cried—and no matter how many takes we went through, Michael still ended up in tears. Finally, Spielberg decided to use one of the takes in which Michael's voice audibly breaks with the force of his emotion.

Michael described the resulting album. "It's a special package with a beautiful storybook so that people can read along as I narrate the story. There are sound effects from the movie and you can hear the voice of E.T. in the background. I sing a special song that was written for the album, and Quincy Jones is doing the music."

Unfortunately, this project ran into legal snags as soon as it was released. It had been recorded on the MCA label, through a deal made by Spielberg, and Michael had gotten permission from Epic, with whom he had an exclusive contract, to participate in the project on the condition that the album would not be released until early 1983. But somehow — funny how these accidents do happen — *E.T.* came out in November 1982, in time for the lucrative Christmas sales period. Epic cried foul. They went to court to get an injunction against the continued distribution of the album, claiming that it misled purchasers into thinking they were buying a new Michael Jackson solo album. The courts agreed, and with only about 450,000 albums sold, *E.T.* was pulled off the market.

But the bad luck of the *E.T.* album didn't keep Steven Spielberg and Michael Jackson from thinking about working together again, and it has been rumored ever since that Spielberg is personally writing a script for a forthcoming film to star Michael Jackson. What's it to be about? Well, it's a strong possibility that it will be the retelling of another favorite children's story: *Peter Pan*.

If you can believe what you read in print, the person responsible for urging Michael to play Peter Pan was none other than Jane Fonda. Jane and Michael met at a Hollywood party and became friends, and that led to Michael's making a visit to the set of *On Golden Pond*. Jane recalls, "I remember driving with him one day, and I said, 'God, Michael, I wish I could find a movie I could produce for you.' And suddenly I knew. I said, 'I know what you've got to do. It's *Peter Pan.*' Tears welled up in his eyes and he said, 'Why did you say that?' with this *ferocity.* I said, 'I realize *you're* Peter Pan.' And he started to cry and said, 'You know, all over the walls of my room are pictures of Peter Pan. I've ready everything that Barrie wrote. I totally identify with Peter Pan, the lost boy of never-never land.' " Jane added, "Oh, I can see him, leading lost children into a world of fantasy and magic."

Whether or not the film Spielberg does with Michael Jackson turns out to be Peter Pan or not remains to be seen . . . although the subject does seem to be particularly appropriate to Michael. But it does appear to be certain that they will do a film together and it seems even more certain that, whatever it is, it will be a big box-office success. Meanwhile, Michael occupies himself with picking up tips on acting from his many friends and admirers in the business. The list is absolutely amazing. It includes not just Jane Fonda, Diana Ross, Tatum O'Neal and her father Ryan. There's also Katharine Hepburn—yes, *the* Katharine Hepburn. She met him while he was visiting the set of *On Golden Pond,* and became such a Michael Jackson fan that she was later spotted in attendance at one of his concerts. Always generous with her time when it comes to helping talented young people, she has spent hours talking to him about acting technique.

Another veteran who took Michael under his wing was Hepburn's co-star, Henry Fonda. Fonda took him out fishing and spoke to him about the way an actor meets various challenges, on the screen and in the theater. Two shy people, they became very close—so close that Michael rushed to Fonda's house the night he died, to sit with his widow and children, almost as if he had been part of the family.

Michael has friends in a younger generation of stars as well. There is Sidney Poitier, John Travolta, Kristy McNichol. Fred Astaire, who is one of Michael's idols (and also one of his influences) talks to him frequently by phone. Liza Minelli is another good friend, as is *Fame's* Debbie Allen.

With help from friends like these, Michael Jackson's next film should be a smash!

5

MICHAEL'S SOLO CAREER

The very first reviews of the Jackson Five speculated dubiously about what the future might hold for a group of cute black kids whose music appealed primarily to the bubble-gum set. Most of the predictions were gloomy, but there was one exception: It was generally agreed that whatever happened to the Jacksons as a group, Michael was a good bet for a long career as a solo artist.

Well, they were wrong about the fate of the Jackson Five, but they were certainly right about Michael. Today his solo career is the most successful in the world.

Michael's first solo effort was an album he

made back in 1972, called *Got To Be There*. The idea of a solo album for Michael came primarily from Motown. They wanted to capitalize on his popularity as the lead singer of the Jackson Five; and they may also have intended a hedge for the future, in case it turned out to be true that the Jackson Five would lose their audience once they all grew up.

They turned Michael over to veteran Motown producer Hal Davis, and the ubiquitous "Corporation," and waited to see what would happen. What did was a hit single, a successful album, and an award for Male Vocalist of the Year. Quite a feat for a thirteen-year-old boy's debut album.

The single was "Got To Be There," a bouncy love song. *Rolling Stone*'s Vince Aletti commented, "On 'Got To Be There,' Michael's voice echoes and swirls, whispers and cries out with this unbelievable purity: OOh, what a feeling there'll be/the moment she says she loves me. It's a weird combination of innocence and utter professionalism, real feeling and careful calculation, that's fascinating and finally irresistible." The single made it all the way to the Number One spot on the charts, as hordes of teenyboppers fueled their daydreams of a romance with Michael Jackson.

Another single from this album also did well, and has since become a Jackson standard at concerts, and that was "Rockin' Robin." Later, one more cut from the album got airplay as a single, "I Wanna Be Where You Are." Aletti characterized it as a "supreme production, with shouting from Michael that equals his early work and a finish that always has me screaming loud enough to alarm the neighbors." The critic concluded, "Even the inconsequential songs on Michael's album have their appeal." All in all, it was an impressive first solo performance. His peers in the music business agreed, a fact which they demonstrated by voting him the Best Male Vocalist of the Year on the strength of his performance on *Got To Be There.*

Motown was never a company to refrain from striking when the iron was hot. Not only did they set in motion another album, but they arranged for Michael to sing the theme song for a movie that was expected to appeal to the same young people who bought his records. The movie was *Ben,* a low-budget horror flick that was well calculated to appeal to the fantasies of prepubescents. The hero is a boy who is spurned by his classmates. His scheme for revenge on the whole heartless world involves breeding ferocious rats who are going to do his bidding. The leader is a large rat named Ben, who becomes the boy's best friend.

As you can tell from this brief plot summary, the title song, "Ben," an ode to the boy's rat friend, could easily turn into terrible bathos or a bad joke. But Michael Jackson brought to this little ballad his own special quality of innocence and belief, and he made it a touching experience. Critic Vince Aletti admitted that Michael's delivery of the lines "They don't see you as I do/I wish they would try to" tore him up every time he heard it. Michael's rendition of this title song became a hit single; he was asked to sing it at the Academy Award presentation; and Motown also made it the title song of his next album, which features a picture of Michael and a rat on the cover. The title song more or less carried the album, which had no other hit single and no particularly memorable songs in the Michael Jackson canon.

Michael didn't make another solo album until early in 1975. Motown decided to turn their young star over to one of their most successful producers, Brian Holland. He had worked for Motown in the early years, and was largely responsible for the sound of the Supremes; then he left to form his own production company, Holland-Dozier-Holland Production, Inc. Now he had signed a contract with Motown for a return engagement, to produce a new album for the Supremes, one for the Jackson Five (*Moving Violation*) and a solo album for Michael.

The album was called *Forever, Michael*. It tries to build on Michael's more mature voice and his more mainstream style (this was about the time that the Jacksons were appearing in

Vegas and at Radio City Music Hall.) There is some difference of opinion about the result.

Some people felt that the album was artistically successful, even though neither of its two singles had the sales one might expect for a star of Michael's magnitude. This school of thought blames the album's commercial insignificance on the fact that it was released after the Jacksons had announced the move to Epic. They point out that Motown had neither the motive nor the inclination to promote the album the way they had his past productions. Vince Aletti described "Just a Little Bit of You," one of the singles released, as "a wonderfully bouncy, romantic prescription with a driving intro and cascades of violins that put Barry White and MFSB to shame." The other single was "Dear Michael," a saccharine little ballad based on an imaginary letter from a fan who closed by predicting sadly that he'll never ever see her letter; Michael responds by saying he is dreaming of meeting her and signs himself, "Forever, Michael." It *is* all a bit too cute, although as usual Michael manages to put the lyrics over with convincing sincerity.

The other school of thought denounced *Forever, Michael* as a flop because it was too slick, too pop, too far away from Michael's roots. The reviewer for *High Fidelity* complained that the album had gone too far into the middle-of-the-road. "Yes, Jackson is an expert ballad singer; yes, this disc with its many famous producers, is slicker than slick; yes, it is attractive and entertaining. Nevertheless, I object to this conventional treatment of an unconventional talent. The desouling of Michael Jackson may be one way to lengthen his career. But it's a sad route to take."

Now that we can view *Forever, Michael* within the context of Michael Jackson's career to date, it seems a natural step in his evolution into the mainstream of popular music. His first two albums drew heavily on the rhythm-and-blues background that had been the foundation of the Jackson Five's musical experience; Motown contributed an element of slickly packaged soul. But if Michael Jackson had simply continued to record in that mold, he would have appealed to a limited audience—mostly blacks—and he would have failed to grow artistically. Already, in his earlier songs such as "Ben," "Got To Be There," and "We've Got a Good Thing Going," Michael had proved conclusively that he was capable of putting across a ballad, handling material that touched the audience emotionally—often at the very same moment that it made them want to dance. On *Forever, Michael,* he simply extended this range with cuts like the title song, "Take Me Back," and "One Day in Your Life." As a whole, the album is perhaps a bit too slick, a bit too glitzy. But it was a necessary step along the

Here is Michael at the age of thirteen—already a seasoned pro and the heartthrob of a lot of young ladies. (Syndication International/Photo Trends)

The Jackson Five, plus Randy, leave London after a command performance for the Queen. From left to right: Marlon, Michael, Randy, Jackie, Jermaine, and Tito. (Syndication International/Photo Trends)

Young Michael attends a gala event in black tie and tux with his father, Joe Jackson, for many years Michael's manager. (Jerry Watson/Photo Trends)

Michael doesn't seem to be the least bit afraid of Lobo, the Jacksons' guard dog, trained to chase intruders off the grounds. (Doris Nieh/Photo Trends)

The Jacksons, minus Jermaine and plus Randy, now a full-fledged member. By this time Michael was "big and cute"; he's second from the right. (Epic Records)

On their way to the opening of *The Wiz*, here's Michael with the most special lady in his life, his mom, Katherine Jackson. (Derek/Photo Trends)

Michael plays the Scarecrow, trapped on his perch as the chorus of crows taunt him. Soon he'll jump down and wobble around in a wonderful dance that was one of the highlights of *The Wiz*. (Universal City Studios)

Here's the Michael Jackson dancing style early in his career; this picture was taken during his appearance on a television special called "Marlo Thomas and Friends in Free to Be . . . You and Me." (ABC)

(Photo Trends)

Here's the Michael Jackson dance style of today . . . a much more sophisticated but no less energetic performance. (Movie Star News)

Michael Jackson and Paul McCartney take a break in the recording studio to clown for the camera. They are, of course, in the process of turning out a hit. (Columbia Records)

Michael introduces writer Neil Murray to his pet boa constrictor, Muscles. The affectionate snake provides the title for the hit Michael wrote for Diana Ross. (Syndication International/Photo Trends)

Michael Jackson with his new look of the Eighties.

Diana Ross, a leading lady in Michael's life, congratulates him on winning seven American Music Awards in early 1984. (United Press International)

Michael and Jane Fonda, his special friend, display their records at a press conference. Hers has just been issued; his, *Thriller*, has gone double platinum. (AP/Wide World Photos)

Two weeks after his burning accident, Michael attends a CBS party in New York's Museum of Natural History. (Cortery/Sygma)

Michael flanked by Brooke and Emmanuel Lewis (*Webster*), two of his guests at the Grammy Awards. (Sam Emerson/Sygma)

February 28, 1984: Michael, with twelve Grammys in the offing, arrives backstage with a radiant Brooke Shields at the 26th annual Grammy Awards presentation in Los Angeles. (AP/Wide World Photos)

Michael with his eight Grammy Awards and without his sunglasses—removed for the benefit of "the girls in the balcony". (United Press International)

way to the pop sound eventually perfected by Michael Jackson that is a fusion of pop romanticism with the driving beat of dance music.

Right after Michael left Motown, that record label brought out its last Michael Jackson album, *The Best of Michael Jackson.* It went back into the Jackson catalog to pull out some of Michael's hottest songs, both with and without the Jackson Five. Considering the small amount of promotion it received, it sold reasonably well—but basically the album was created without the involvement of Michael.

The next step for Michael's growth as a recording artist came when the Jacksons were finally able to write and produce their own music, in the creation of the *Destiny* album. Michael had been writing songs steadily for several years, but this was his first chance to work them out in the recording studio, to try to advance them from the sound in his head to the same sound on the master tape. He co-wrote with brother Randy the hit song "Shake Your Body (Down to the Ground)" and he also was responsible for its unusual sound. Arranger and keyboard player Greg Phillinganes remembers being impressed by the originality of the effects Michael finally produced, especially toward the end of the song, when vocals and most instruments fade out, to leave only the insistent rhythm of the synthesizer bass and drums to carry the dancers through to the end of the record. He told a reporter, "The long instrumental tag on 'Shake' was totally their idea. I played on the record, but hadn't heard the final version. Michael handed me a copy of the test pressing and with his big smile said, 'Listen to this.' Well, it was hot!"

Another song on *Destiny* that is significant in Michael's career development is the tune called "Bless His Soul," written by Michael and (he now confirms) written *about* him as well. Here we begin for the first time to penetrate into the inner world of Michael Jackson, where innocence and the desire to love are threatened by the acts of a hostile world—or the fear of that hostility. One verse, for example, goes, "Sometimes I cry cause I'm confused/Is this a fact of being used?/There is no life for me at all/Cause I give myself at beck and call." Subsequently in his solo albums (and especially in *Thriller*) Michael would continue to explore this inner territory, exposing some basic uneasiness about the intentions of the world in which he must live—a feeling that obviously strikes a chord in many of his listeners.

Destiny gave Michael a chance to hone his skills in songwriting and record producing, but he was still looking for more creative freedom. Recording with a group—even when they're all your brothers and have worked with you for more than a decade—is always slightly confining, because things must be agreed upon jointly, worked out ahead of time, altered to allow for the strengths and weaknesses of the group members. Michael felt it was time for another solo album.

And when he met Quincy Jones while acting in *The Wiz,* he knew he had found the right producer to work with. The two of them had hit it off from the very start. Quincy told a reporter, "Michael's a truth machine. He's got a balance between the wisdom of a 60-year-old and the enthusiasm of a child." And Michael in his turn respected Quincy's professional accomplishments. Quincy was a trumpet player who had once played with the great Ray Charles band. In the 1960s, he began to produce some successful pop singles (one of the best known is "It's My Party" by Leslie Gore). A multi-talented man, he also put together his own jazz band, and did successful live performances and recordings. In the 1970s, he began to get involved in music for films and TV, and was the musical director for *Roots*—and, of course, *The Wiz*.

Quincy Jones had the reputation of a producer who knew how to get what he wanted in the studio. He was identified with a classy, smooth sound; it's the kind of music that sounds simple and relaxed when you first hear it but that later reveals itself to be full of complexity and sophistication. When the executives at Epic heard that Michael wanted "Q" to produce his next album, they all became a bit nervous. How would Michael's raw energy and rhythm-and-blues-based music mesh with Quincy's jazz sounds and smooth veneer?

The answer turned out to be, very well. The album that they created together, called *Off the Wall,* was an unprecedented hit. It sold over seven million copies worldwide (*Destiny,* which Epic certainly regarded as a success, in comparison sold a mere one million copies). Two singles from the album made it to the Number One spot—"Don't Stop 'Til You Get Enough," and "Rock With You." Two others also made it to the Top Ten: "Off the Wall" and "She's Out of My Life." This total of four hit singles from one album was a record for a solo album (it had been equalled just once before by a group, Fleetwood Mac, with their monster album *Rumours.*) Just for good measure, Michael threw in a fifth song that became a top-selling single in the UK, although never in the US: "Girlfriend." Michael also won a Grammy for Best Male Rhythm and Blues Performer for his vocal on "Don't Stop 'Til You Get Enough."

Off the Wall was released at a time that the record business seemed to be going into a slump, and it was one of the few bright spots on the financial horizon for many record-store owners during 1979 and 1980. In fact, it continued to sell throughout 1981, and was voted most popular soul album for that year by readers of *Cash Box,* a music-business trade paper. But its success was not limited to its commercial aspect alone. Most critics agreed that it was an artistic triumph—for Michael Jackson as well as all the other musicians who worked with him.

Once again Michael Jackson demonstrated his talent as a songwriter. He wrote the hit "Don't Stop 'Til You Get Enough," which is one of the best pieces of dance music ever created. An interesting sidelight on Michael's method of writing this type of song, in which the rhythm is such an integral part of the effect, is that he says he writes on piano and drum—an unusual approach, but perhaps it helps to explain his ultimate success. For many songwriters, the beat is something that is added later, often at the behest of an arranger or producer who is trying to flesh out the melody and chord structure that the writer has come up with. In Michael's case, through his use of the drum, that all-important element of the beat is already there, worked in and around the words and the music. It assures that the lyrics "speak" the right way, that the phrases of the melody start and end in the right places, that the entire composition is propelled by the beat rather than merely adorned by it.

Michael wrote another cut on the album as well, "Working Day and Night." Gerri Hirshey, writing about Michael in *Rolling Stone,* commented aptly that this song could only have been written by a dancer. Its sense of pace is truly incredible, and it's true that it does seem to have built into it those places for just the right spin, or twist, or funky little rhythm step, that give a dance its punctuation.

Other writers helped with *Off the Wall* too. Both the title cut and the other big hit, "Rock With You" were written by Rod Temperton, (formerly a member of Heat Wave and also the writer of George Benson's big hit, "Give Me the Night"). Temperton also contributed "Burn This Disco Out," a good piece of dance music. Paul McCartney was another contributor, penning the song "Girlfriend" which was such a success in the UK.

Of course, the song itself is only the beginning. The real challenge is putting it over—singing it in a way that makes the listener *hear* the lyrics and feel the melody and beat. And no one in the world is better than Michael Jackson at either of these tasks. Part of his effectiveness comes from the fact that it is obvious that he is himself strongly affected by the song. He told one reporter that when he sang "Don't Stop 'Til You Get Enough," he felt touched by a force within. "The thing that touches me is very special. It's a message I have to tell. I start crying and the pain is wonderful. It's amazing. It's like God."

And Quincy Jones remembers the struggle he had because of Michael's involvement with the music on one particular cut, the beautiful and sad ballad, "She's Out of My Life." He said, "I had a song I'd been saving for Michael called 'She's Out of My Life' [written by Tom Bahler]. Michael heard it, and it clicked. But when he sang it, he would cry. Every time we did it, I'd look up at the end and Michael would be crying. I said, 'We'll come back in two weeks and do it again, and maybe it won't tear you up so much.' Came back and he started to get teary. So we left it in." Clearly, when the singer feels the mood of the song so strongly, the listener is going to be drawn into that emotion. And Michael, because he seems to be such a believer himself, so totally devoid of cynicism, can virtually make an audience share his tears.

Off the Wall also marked another step in Michael's development as a producer, since he continued on this album to be involved in the process that turns a song into a finished recording. Quincy Jones praised his willingness to work and learn: "He does his homework and rehearses and works hard at home. Most singers want to do everything in the studio. They're lazy . . . When he commits to an idea, he goes all the way with it . . . It's a long way from idea to execution. Everybody wants to go to heaven and nobody wants to die." Michael was an exception — and an exception especially rare among singers.

The way modern studio recordings are made tends to encourage a singer to remain uninvolved with the rest of the music. Commonly, the producer and/or arranger begin the process with a group of studio musicians. They start by having a piano player beat out the rhythm and the melody and anybody who feels like it singing the vocal part; this is captured on one track of the tape—and later erased. Then, as the musicians listen to this skeleton tape, they begin to lay down tracks on top of it. Usually the drums and bass go first, then the keyboards, then lead instrumentals, such as the guitar breaks, or the wailing saxophone, or the synthesizer tricks. Each of these instruments will probably be recorded on a separate track, which makes it easy to replace or rework any of them (and is quite feasible in the modern recording studio with its 32- or even 48-track capacity).

Once the entire instrumental part of the recording is more or less complete, the star vocalist comes into the studio—often without a single live musician in there with him. He puts on the big earphones and listens to the music that has already been created. Then he simply sings along with it, and his work is done. He goes home to count his future royalties and autograph his glossies.

Meanwhile, back in the studio, the producer

and the engineer mix the master tape, making critical decisions about how loud each instrumental track should be, how much treble or bass on each single instrument, how far above the instrumental the vocal should be pitched. They may decide to make some changes, by re-recording an instrumental part, overdubbing another instrument, hiring some back-up singers to thicken up the vocal texture, inserting an echo here, a fadeout there. In short, using the raw material of the taped tracks, they create the album. Then they send a test pressing to the star, who listens to it a few times to find out what's on it and then runs out to tell everyone about "my" new record.

But with Michael Jackson, things are very different. To begin with, he has written some of the songs. In the second place, he has jammed with the musicians who are going to play on the record to get some musical ideas stirred up, and then he has rehearsed with them to work those ideas out. He is likely to be in the studio while they record their tracks — and if he isn't, he is going to have those tracks messengered right over to his house, where he will listen to them in his own recording studio to decide what works and what doesn't. By the time he actually begins to record himself, he is thoroughly in command of the musical creation. And then he will sit in the studio for hours listening to the mixing process, helping to decide what the final sound should be. Once there is a final master tape, Michael will also be involved in checking the test pressing for quality and fidelity, approving the album cover and sleeve, reading over the promotional material and the planned advertising for the album. In fact, he will continue to monitor all the activities involved in marketing and selling the album, right up until the day when he checks over his accountants audit of Epic's records of number of copies of the album sold and royalties due.

Anyone who has worked with him has come to recognize that, professionally, Michael Jackson is in full control. Steven Spielberg elucidated, "Sometimes he appears to other people to be sort of wavering on the fringes of twilight, but there is great conscious forethought behind everything he does. He's very smart about his career and the choices he makes." And Greg Phillinganes, who once again worked with Michael as keyboardist on *Off The Wall,* spoke more specifically about the way Michael collaborated in the studio with producer Quincy Jones. "Their ideas just blend into each other. You see, Michael is not like a lot of other singers who come around just to add a vocal. Michael is involved in the whole album. 'Q' is basically an overseer who runs the show without really running the show."

Off the Wall was a major triumph for Michael Jackson. The album stayed on the Top

Ten for nearly eight months, and altogether made the charts for 84 weeks. It went platinum in the US, UK, Australia, and Canada; in Holland it merely went gold. And it spawned five hit singles worldwide. For some artists, such an album would be the highlight of a lifetime. But for Michael, it was just a warm-up for bigger things to come.

For the next two years, Michael put most of his working time into the Jacksons, making the album *Triumph* and going out on tour with a show that was largely his own creation. But by 1982, he was ready to work on his own again.

He began the year by writing a song for his friend Diana Ross. Titled *Muscles,* it was downright steamy in its sexuality, a woman's plea for a great male body to hold on to. (Amusingly, the title is also the name of Michael's pet boa constrictor, a great body that wants to hold onto *you.*) When he brought the song to Diana, she loved its theatricality, but told Michael she would record it on one condition only: that he act as producer of the song. He suggested that they should co-produce it, but she stood firm in demanding that he should take full responsibility in the studio. He agreed, they made the record, it was released as a single. It was a shot in the arm for Diana's recording career, and became a hit on both the pop and the rhythm-and-blues charts.

Before he turned to work on his own new

solo album, Michael took the time to record another collaboration, this time with Paul McCartney. He sang a duet with Paul on a tune called "Say, Say, Say," and another one, "The Man." Both were contained on Paul's new album, and "Say, Say, Say" was released as a single (in 1983) that made the charts in both the US and the UK. While he and Paul were working together, they went on to cut a track for Michael's new album as well. The song was called "The Girl is Mine" and it's an argument between Paul and Michael over the affections of a young lady.

With the work with Paul behind him, it was time for Michael to settle down and do the hard work to create his next solo album, to be called *Thriller*. Once again, he chose to have Quincy Jones produce the album—why quarrel with success?—and Quincy also contributed one song that he co-wrote, "PYT (Pretty Young Thing)"; it was recorded with Michael's sisters LaToya and Janet singing back-up. Rod Temperton was back too, writing the title song as well as two other tracks on the album, "The Lady in My Life" and "Baby Be Mine." But in addition to going back to the people who helped make *Off the Wall* such a success, Michael also brought in some new musical talent. The rock group Toto plays back-up on several cuts, and one of their members, Steve Porcaro, co-wrote the strong song "Human Nature." Drummer

Ndugu Chanceler came in to lay down a drum track on "Billie Jean," and heavy-metal guitarist Eddie Van Halen agreed to contribute a long solo on "Beat It." The master of horror, Vincent Price, dropped by to tape a silly horror rap for the conclusion of *Thriller.* This willingness to collaborate with other well-known artists, to ask them to contribute the things they do best, is the mark of a mature artist.

Michael himself wrote three of the songs on *Thriller,* and they too are a sign of his continuing development as an artist. What's interesting about all three of them is the way they combine a bouncy upbeat rhythm with lyrics that are darkly brooding, even paranoid, in their feeling. "Beat It" is a song about gang warfare, and it seems to explore man's potential for violence. The singer keeps advocating peace — "Don't wanna see no blood" — but it is obvious that others are thrusting violence upon him. In "Billie Jean," he talks about a paternity suit of which the singer is the victim; again, it seems that other people are creating situations that the singer finds intolerable — and inescapable. "Wanna Be Startin' Somethin' " is perhaps the most explicit of the three songs, with its denunciation of gossiping tongues and its acknowledgement of their power to hurt the singer. The singer calls himself a "buffet," a "vegetable" — in other words, something to be devoured by others, all of whom have hostile motives. Lyrics like these suggest that being Michael Jackson is not, despite the money and the success, all fun and games. But the artistry lies not in the complaint, but in Michael's ability to fuse the complaint with the music and to create something that simultaneously makes you dance and makes you think.

When it came to recording the three songs he wrote himself, Michael shared production chores with Quincy Jones. For the rest of the cuts, he was, as usual, deeply involved with the creation of the record, but Quincy was once again the person with ultimate control. There is no question but that *Thriller* is a heavily produced album—the creation of countless hours spent manipulating tracks in the studio rather than the spontaneous effort of a group of musicians getting together to play something. But the net effect is still one of simplicity. The complexity and sophistication are there, but they are not intrusive. A perfect example can be seen in the drum sound in "Billie Jean." According to drummer Chanceler, "Michael always knew how he wanted it to sound. There was originally just a drum machine track on it. I came in and cut a live drum track over the overdub, so that at times during the record there is just me and then the two together." To the casual listener, all that is apparent is the steady rhythmic shuffle. But the variety of that sound appeals to more sophisticated listeners and — just as important — it makes the song hold up under frequent playing, whereas a simple drum machine alone might get monotonous after you'd heard it a few times.

This ability to stand up under repeated listening is no doubt one he strengths of *Thriller* and one of the reasons that it has been so phenomenally successful. The numbers tell the story. *Thriller* was the best-selling album of 1983, selling (to date) nearly 25 million copies worldwide — and still, as of this writing, in the Number One spot. Perhaps even more amazing is the fact that six — yes, *six,* — of the songs on the album have become best-selling singles. This record is unprecedented; and when you consider that the album has only nine songs on it to begin with, you realize that two-thirds of the songs are singles hits!

Thriller has been a truly international success. The album went platinum in the US, Canada, UK, Holland, Australia, New Zealand, Japan, Germany, France, Sweden, Belgium, Switzerland, Spain, Greece, and South Africa; it went gold in Denmark, Italy, Israel, and Norway.

And its success is not just financial, but artistic as well. John Rockwell characterized *Thriller* as a "wonderful pop record" and "another signpost on the road to Michael Jackson's own artistic fulfillment." Vince Aletti, who has been covering Michael Jackson from the very beginning of his career, said, "Here, Quincy gracefully opens the door and the real Michael Jackson steps through: Mr. Entertainment. Obviously, Michael's been honing his art along with his ambition and the result is remarkably sharp, intensely focused . . ." It was widely agreed that Michael's achievement on the album put him in the category of major pop artists.

And *Thriller*'s success also had a major impact on the record industry. Some people go so far as to claim that Michael has rejuvenated the music business. The enormous profitability of *Thriller* has made the record companies bullish again, willing to risk money discovering new artists and developing old ones, in the hope of finding another *Thriller*. Moreover, retailers believe that the sales of *Thriller* created additional sales as well; people who came into the record stores to buy the Michael Jackson album frequently picked up something else while they were there.

But it's not just in record sales alone that Michael Jackson has pointed the way to the future. It is also in synthesizing a new appeal to a wider music audience. For black artists, the success of both of Michael's albums is encouraging, because it proves that black performers can sell records in large quantities — a question that many people in the record business used to debate. And it means that music with its roots in the black community can appeal to everyone. Back in the heyday of Motown, and in the early days of rock, black music was recognized to have a wide appeal. But somehow things changed again in the 1970s, and black performers began to fade away, as their sounds were taken over by white players (especially English groups) and the origins of the sounds were forgotten. Although Michael Jackson's stage persona is not sterotypically black, his music remains firmly within the black tradition that was his own starting point. A professor of political science who was interviewed in the *New York Times,* Marshall Berman, called Michael the "Al Jolson of the 80s . . . Like Al Jolson, he's bringing black music to a white audience. And like Jolson, he shows that you can come out of the ghetto and if you have the energy, you can do anything. It's the American dream."

Michael's mastery of the American dream has had its good effect on other black musicians. Such performers as Prince and Eddie Grant find that it's much easier to get airplay than it used to be, that there's more interest in an indigenous black sound outside what used to be a limited black audience.

Another aspect of Michael's synthesis of several different styles of music is that the singles hits from *Thriller* have been played on a lot of different kinds of radio stations. Of course they were big hits on the dance-oriented stations, found in the large cities and having as their primary market urban, black young people. But they've also been played on AOR (Album Oriented Rock) stations that have traditionally limited themselves to heavy rock performers and ignored pop and disco releases. An exec of Epic Records confirmed that *Thriller* got a lot of airplay on AOR stations and that it was the first time any Michael Jackson music had made it on those stations. With today's new "narrowcasting" approach to radio, station profits have gone up but performers' opportunites have declined. Many stations are locked into rigid formulas that make it impossible for any artist to move outside his or her "assigned" category. With *Thriller,* Michael Jackson reminded station programming directors that their categories are to a great extent artificial and that good music can appeal to everyone. A lot of other artists stand to benefit from this reminder.

Can Michael Jackson top *Thriller?* On the face of it, it would seem virtually impossible. But a new album is already in the planning stages. Nothing is yet definite, but Michael has been talking about some new collaborations that will take him even farther into new territory. He wants to record a duet with Freddie Mercury, the lead singer of *Queen;* he wants to work with Barbra Streisand and with

Johnny Mathis; he'll probably work again with Paul McCartney and with Toto.

And he's still writing songs . . . and moving deeper and deeper inside himself to do it. In fact, he says that many of his songs come to him in dreams, springing up from the deep well of the unconscious. "I wake up from dreams and go, 'Wow, put *this* down on paper.' The whole thing is strange. You hear the words, everything is right there in front of your face. And you say to yourself, 'I'm sorry, I just didn't write this. It's there already.' That's why I hate to take credit for the songs I've written. I feel that somewhere, someplace, it's been done and I'm just a courier bringing it into the world."

Well, wherever he gets his inspirations, they're still coming. And the chances are that by the time they reach the audience in the form of an album, Michael's talent and hard work will have turned it into another hit-studded production. You can count on it, Michael won't stop 'til he gets enough!

6

THE KING OF VIDEOS

The album *Thriller* can certainly stand on its own as a successful artistic creation. But many observers of the highly competitive world of pop music believe that a strong element of that album's commercial success was the release of the promotional videos made to accompany it. There were three of them; and collectively, they demonstrate that Michael Jackson has been an innovative pioneer in the field of videos.

The first video made to promote *Thriller* was one based on the song "Billie Jean." It was directed by Steve Barron, whose previous credits all came from the glitzy arena of prime-time advertising spots — the kind of training that

117

emphasizes the fact that every single second counts. The "Billie Jean" video was filmed in London, and its cost has been estimated at $60,000. That's a lot of money to spend on something that amounts to a promotional give-away. But Michael Jackson, who financed the video himself and owns all the rights to it, felt that the expense was worth it. From the very start, he intended to create something truly unusual and memorable.

The video to "Billie Jean" adds a new level of interpretation to the lyrics of the song. The story line seems to be about the schemes of a lying woman who tries to entangle the singer in a paternity suit: one more instance of the encroachment of a hostile world on the innocence of the singer. The evocative video then complicates the issue further. On the one hand, it emphasizes the singer's innocence and other-worldliness. He walks down the street in a halo of eerie white light, and everything that he touches takes on a brief and miraculous glow. The hostility of the world is visually symbolized by a shadowy detective who is trailing the singer—watching, recording, attempting to photograph his every move. But it turns out that one of his moves is to climb into bed beside a woman—which certainly suggests that there might be some truth to the accusation of paternity.

The denouement depicts the triumph of a

magical creature, which is what we now understand the singer to be. The detective tries to photograph him in bed with the woman, but the sheet that had covered him simply collapses and simultaneously glows. The police then come to arrest the detective, and as he is taken away, we see one last time the glow that means the invisible singer is victoriously taking his leave. The elements of science fiction/fantasy are strongly marked, yet the video is unquestionably also a deeper probe into the meaning of the lyrics of "Billie Jean."

Tom Carson, writing in the *Village Voice*, points out that the goal of most videos is recontextualization—making the audience see the content of a song in some new light. The "Billie Jean" video makes the song at once more disturbing and more confusing.

Michael's second video, made as a promotional piece for "Beat It," serves the opposite function. It clarifies for us the situation that is expressed in the song. "Beat It" seems to be about impending gang warfare, and from the lyrics alone, it seems that the singer will inevitably be drawn into the violence, even if it is against his will. This conflict between the peacefulness of the singer's intentions and the apparently inescapable violence that lies ahead of him is enhanced by the strong rhythms and noisy aggressiveness of the music.

But the video recasts the singer. He is no

longer a reluctant participant in gang warfare but instead a dedicated peacemaker. The opening shows the gangs collecting on the street, while the singer feebly lies in bed. The leaders of the two gangs begin a knife fight, and then the singer appears on the scene and pulls the fighting leaders apart in a display of great personal power. The conclusion shows the singer leading both gangs as they turn into his enormous chorus line—everyone peacefully dancing together. The video transforms the singer from a slightly wimpy victim of other people's actions into a strong initiator of action himself. And in the end, his peaceful innocence is tougher, smarter, *badder* than the machismo of the gang members.

This subtext of "Beat It" is to a great extent overshadowed by the purely visual delight it creates. The video was filmed on the streets of Watts, and it enlisted the energies and talents of nearly 200 young people from those streets. Several of them are extremely skillful break dancers, who get a few featured moments in the video. But even the anonymous members of the crowd move in a way that is sharp and clearly focused and bursting with vitality. And when Michael himself—in his red leather jacket, jeans, white socks, and low-heeled loafers—gets pumped up, his display of dancing is absolutely dazzling. You can watch this video with no knowledge of the song . . . in fact, you can even watch it without the sound track . . . and still derive enormous pleasure simply from the skill of the dancing, the flash of the colors, the incredible energy that leaps off the screen.

The "Beat It" video was another Michael Jackson Production, and it cost roughly $150,000. The director was Bob Giraldi, another successful creator of television commercials. Michael Peters, who choreographed the Broadway musical *Dream Girls,* was in charge of the dance sequences. And perhaps only Michael, who personally acted as producer, could have pulled off the extraordinary degree of authenticity that is the foundation of this video. Those 200 extras are kids from real street gangs, and they really are feuding with one another. Michael convinced them to work with him, and with one another, and according to reports, he maintained a good rapport with them throughout the period of shooting. He posed for pictures with them, he met their parents, he kissed their girlfriends, he handed out autographed photos. The real-life set actually ran closely parallel to the situation being dramatized: Michael was able to act as peace-maker, at least for a while, between these rival gangs.

The third video created by Michael Jackson was a promotion for the title cut of the album, the song "Thriller"—one with obviously great visual potential. And it was perhaps at this particular point that Michael took the video from promotional gimmick into the realm of art form. It was certainly unnecessary as a promotional device, since the album was already on its way to becoming one of the biggest sellers of all time. And the video's cost, reputed to be well over a million dollars, was too high for it ever to be a cost-effective way of promoting any album. What the "Thriller" video did primarily was establish Michael Jackson as the king of videos, in control of an artform that he made all his own.

You can get some idea of the production values of the "Thriller" video from the statistics. But look also at the talent involved in its creation. The director was John Landis, who was responsible for the spooky *An American Werewolf in London* as well as a segment of the film *The Twilight Zone*. Choreographer Michael Peters was back, and he was directing a cast of eighteen professional dancers. More than twenty makeup artists were used to bring about the startling transformations of the cast into a wild variety of monsters. And the Grand Master of Horror, Vincent Price, made an appearance to intone the campy rap he contributed to the record itself.

The completed video runs for about nine minutes (and was shot in 35 mm. film rather than less expensive videotape.) It begins with the singer out on a date with a beautiful girl (played by Ola Ray). The basic premise is the same as that of the song lyrics, but once again, there is a shift in meaning from the record to the video. In the record, the implication is that the singer is using the terror involved by a horror movie as a pretext for getting close to his date. It's a slightly comic flip side of the nightclub routine Eddie Murphy does, in which he complains about girls who go to horror movies and then keep their eyes closed through the entire movie he's paying for! The singer has found the silver lining in this situation, in the girl's willingness to snuggle up for protection from the movie monsters.

But in the video, the monsters are not confined to the screen. Instead, the movie audience begins to turn into monsters too— even the singer, who seems to cross back and forth from monster to date. Some sharp-tongued women have suggested that "Thriller" accurately depicts the experience of going out on a date with a man you don't know well . . . but it seems unlikely that Michael Jackson intended to make a caustic comment on the unreliability of the blind date. The spirit of the "Thriller" video is that of children in the house of horrors, having a terrific time scaring one another—and themselves—at the same time that they reassures themselves it's only a game.

"Thriller" seems to grow in large measure out of Michael Jackson's love for cinematic special effects. It's another of his fantasies, akin to the fun of being the Scarecrow in Oz or kissing E.T. This time, it's the chance to turn into a monster—albeit a somewhat lovable one—before our very eyes.

All three of Michael's videos were helmed by different directors. But they have in common the fact that they were produced by Michael Jackson, and the internal evidence suggests that they were primarily Michael Jackson creations. He came up with the ideas, as well as many of the visual images; then he brought in an experienced director to help turn his concepts into celluloid reality—just as Quincy Jones helped turn his musical concepts into record albums.

In fact, it appears that videos have currently become Michael Jackson's primary creative outlet. Perhaps it's because for him, the recording studio is no longer an exciting challenge. He's been working there for fifteen years, and certainly by now, the thrill must be gone. But the medium of video is brand new—not only to Michael but to everyone else. It's the perfect arena in which to develop a highly personal style . . . and then, as Michael always drives himself to do, to perfect it.

Michael Jackson's video style is, like his own personal style, a mixture of fantasy, childishness, and ahead-of-the-minute dancing: all slickly packaged with a high gloss veneer. But despite the slickness, the videos are surprisingly effective at evoking an emotional response. Although part of our reaction comes from a reasoned interest in the story line, much of it is linked to the purely visual impact of the images. Watching some of these moments is like hitting your funny bone on the edge of the table. You experience a *frisson* of total response that never travels through the thinking part of the brain but is purely instinctual. An example can be seen in the sight of Michael lying on his bed at the beginning of "Beat It"; we respond to his posture immediately and unthinkingly, with memories of our own hopeless moments. Another example is the slow and gentle collapse of the sheet in "Billie Jean" that symbolizes the defeat of evil schemes in the face of Michael's special powers. Or the somehow friendly glow that Michael emits throughout that video, a visual signal that convinces without argument that Michael is no mere mortal.

In a sense, all these images are based on common childhood fantasies: being invisible, turning into a monster, metamorphosing from puny victim into the most respected boy on the street, defeating the vigilant grownup who is watching us all the time. These speak to our buried daydreams of power, to our wish to be something more than the ordinary powerless child we know, or remember, ourselves to be. Such fantasies about secret powers are well calculated to appeal to the young people who remain one of the major audiences for Michael Jackson's music.

But at the same time, the slick production values make the fantasy acceptable to these young visual connoisseurs. The presentation is anything but childlike—rather, it is the extreme of adult professionalism. This tension between a very sophisticated presentation and a very childish emotional content lies at the heart of much of Michael Jackson's work, and it is surely one of the reasons for his broad appeal.

Of course, one other reason for the enormous success of all three of these videos is simply the outstanding performing ability of Michael Jackson. "Billie Jean" utilizes his considerable talent as an actor. He conveys, primarily by his expressions, the sadness he feels at being watched and followed for malicious reasons. In "Thriller" he shows, by both expression and posture, the eagerness of the young male out on a date, as well as the agreeable thrills of horror experienced in a movie theater. These performances hint at his developing potential as an actor . . . and make fans eager for his next screen appearance.

But it's as a dancer that Michael is most sensational on these videos. Audiences have been impressed with Michael's dancing ability since he was just five years old, and his skills have matured greatly in the past twenty years, as he has become more and more original. Technically, he is amazing, especially in his ability to pull off fast moves and still make them crystal clear. Sometimes it seems that he is doing things impossible for the human body to accomplish: try, for example, whipping your hand back and forth at about half the speed Michael has on "Beat It" and you'll feel like you are in imminent danger of fracturing your wrist. And sometimes his legs scissor the air so quickly that it seems they must snap.

Speed is not his only virtue as a dancer. He also has what professional dancers call "line", which, roughly translated into words, means the ability to extend the body into some graceful position and hold it there, stretched out, long enough for the silhouette to be seen against the backdrop of space. You can see that line in the still photos that have been released from all three of the videos. Each pose is a graceful composition, as fully thought out as an artist's painting: the angle of the arms and legs, the thrust of the head, the diagonal of the torso, the set of the hips. Each of these photographs would make a striking outline, creating a pattern of dark shapes against the light and space of the background.

And, like a good ballet dancer, Michael keeps his line flowing. As he moves from one position to the next, he is conscious of the little interim steps, and he makes each of those as graceful as the final pose. Many dancers (you can see this happen if you watch some of them in the "Beat It" video) are capable of achieving and holding some fabulous pose, but in between these highlights of their performance, they seem to be scurrying around, churning and thrashing as they get themselves ready for the launch into the next striking attitude. Only a great dancer can make that line flow from one pose to the next — and Michael Jackson is one of those greats.

Choreographer Michael Peters, who worked on two of the videos, says that Michael spent a great deal of time studying Fred Astaire's performances in his old movies. Although Michael's dance steps are quite different from Fred Astaire's, the similarity of the style is unmistakable. Both men have the same slim elongated figure, the easy grace, the sense of movement that comes from high up, in the torso, rather than down at the knees or ankles. Perhaps their greatest similarity lies in their identical sense of effortlessness.

It is impossible ever to imagine Fred Astaire getting all hot and bothered from the exertion of dancing — even though we know that in reality most off his routines call for hours of incredibily hard work to capture on film. His genius was to make it all look easy. You don't see his muscles knot up, or the sweat roll of his body; instead, he gently floats across the screen with what appears to be a minimum of effort. Even when he picks Ginger up bodily, or dashes full tilt to the top of the stairs, he makes it look physically easy.

Michael Jackson has exactly the same uncanny ability. His hair may look a bit more disheveled than Fred's — but then it always does, even when he isn't dancing. On his feet, he looks just as effortless. His arms and legs seem to move on some unusual principle . . . one that doesn't require muscle power and a high expenditure of energy. When he spins, it looks like he is energized by a concealed electric motor. Occasionally, Michael dances with his eyes closed, but you know it's not because he has to concentrate on the effort he's making but because he has been transported to some other place of existence.

One other characteristic of Michael Jackson's performing art revealed by these videos is his sense of restraint. Now that may seem like an odd word to use in conjunction with a video that cost more than a million dollars and features a large cast of dancers turning into monsters. Certainly, he likes glossy production numbers, and he is a big fan of special effects. But once they have been created, he uses them judiciously, with genuine restraint — and that makes them doubly effective. You want to see the videos again and again, because you want to see more. Nothing has been overused.

This restraint is characteristic of his dancing as well. He'll work for hours, maybe even days or weeks to perfect some stunning step. And then he will use it once . . . just once . . . no more. Most dancers (and choreographers) are constitutionally incapable of exercising such restraint. When they find a step that's unusual, that makes them look good, that attracts attention, they're going to use it over and over. And if you notice it once in a performance, you can bet you're going to see it again. And again. And again. But with Michael, you wait and you wait, and it never comes again. Instead, you see something new that makes you gasp—and that also will not be repeated. Such restraint is the hallmark of a great artist.

And of a successful performer, since he always leaves the audience longing for more.

In fact, Michael succeeded in building up such an appetite for more than he was able to make an hour-long documentary film, about creating the "Thriller" video, and to sell it to eagerly waiting fans. A Michael Jackson Production, it was called *The Making of "Thriller."* It shows exactly how the video was made, and gives fans a chance to see more of the dancing, more of the elaborate steps . . . more, more, more. Yes, the whole thing amounts to a puff piece about Michael: it includes home movies of little Michael back in Gary, a clip of his rendition of "Billie Jean" at the Motown Reunion, and shots of devoted fans singing his praises. But ask yourself—what other star could produce a puff piece and then sell 100,000 copies of the videocassette at $29.95 apiece? And then go on to sell it for airing on pay-TV?

Michael's videos were trend-setters in other ways too. One of the hottest showcases for music videos is the cable channel MTV. But when Epic's parent company, CBS, went to MTV with Michael's first videos, the programming people turned them down. They thought the MTV audience would tolerate nothing but hard rock; and, some have alleged, they also thought their audiences wanted to see mostly white faces. Whether it was the result of a deliberate policy or not, the fact of the matter was that black artists were not getting airplay on MTV. Nor were musicians who didn't fall into the clear-cut category of hard rock. Gossip has it that CBS brought some heavy pressure to bear on MTV, and that the record company's president threatened to withdraw all CBS videos from MTV. Both sides officially deny this story, but most observers think that some kind of struggle did take place. MTV finally agreed to show Michael's "Beat It" video—and it promptly became one of the most popular works they'd ever aired.

The results of this airing were first felt in the sales of the album *Thriller*. As Robert Christgau summed it up in the *Village Voice,* "With MTV fallen, AOR jumped in after the top 40 and black radio, and a hit album was transformed into an unprecedented megacrossover." The subsequent release of videos for "Billie Jean" and "Thriller" only fanned the flames for Michael's hot album—and who knows, without the videos, whether it would have been the incredible success it turned out to be?

But it wasn't Michael Jackson alone who benefited from cracking the MTV market. In his wake, both the cable channel and the MTV imitators that have sprung up as syndicated shows on regular channels all show videos by black performers. Eddie Grant, Natalie Cole, Evelyn King, James Ingram, Prince, and others are finally able to get airplay.

Robert Christgau astutely pointed out one other, not so happy, effect of the success of Michael Jackson's videos—and that is that they once again create an extremely high price tag for a shot at a hit record in the competitive music business. With recent technological innovations, the cost of recording time in a competent studio has come down significantly, and that gave artists with a bankroll of only $10,000-$20,000 the chance to cut a decently engineered record and themselves promote it to regional success, hoping it would then be picked up nationally and become a major hit. And the first videos that were created as record promos did little to undermine that possibility. They were low-budget productions that often required no more than hiring someone to shoot some footage of the musicians at work, perhaps utilizing a few fancy camera angles and a couple of computer tricks as they put the final tape together.

Of course, few artists are going to emulate Michael Jackson and spend as much as a million dollars on a video. But his success has visibly upped the ante. Now it seems that no group is going to get radio play or store orders unless they have a video that will be seen on TV. And to get there, the video has to be slickly produced, with a name director, some sort of a script, perhaps a few special effects, the hiring of some actors to appear along with the musicians. All of this costs $50,000 at a minimum, and $200,000 videos are becoming more and more common. Once again, it has become virtually impossible for any musician to make it big without a contract from a major record label.

The widespread appeal of Michael Jackson's videos has simply confirmed his unique place in the world of pop music. Charlie Kendall, the program director of one of New York City's most popular rock radio stations, recently summed it all up for the *New York Times:* "Michael Jackson is mass culture, not pop culture—he appeals to everybody. No one can deny that he's got a tremendous voice and plenty of style and that he can dance like a demon. He appeals to all ages and he appeals to every kind of pop listener. This kind of performer comes once in a generation."

7

MICHAEL SWEEPS THE GRAMMY AWARDS

Once a year, for the past 26 years, the members of the Recording Academy have honored the music and the musicians that they think are the best of the year's crop of recordings. Initially, it was a fairly quiet — you might even say obscure — event. But in recent years, it has moved onto television and become a glamorous, star-studded occasion. As entertainment, the Grammy Awards is more successful than any of its counterparts in other fields, such as the Emmys or the Oscars, perhaps because the musicians are younger, freer, and more used to adlibbing in front of huge crowds.

The awards for records played during 1983 were made on February 28, 1984. More than 60,000,000 people watched the whole thing on television. Although it was ostensibly a night to pay tribute to all of the best recording artists, in actual fact, the whole thing boiled down to the music industry's tribute to Michael Jackson and the unbelievable success of his album *Thriller*. As Mickey Rooney, one of the presenters, told the glittering audience of artists and record-company executives, "It's a pleasure doing the Michael Jackson show."

The evening was an extraordinary personal and professional triumph for Michael Jackson; and as he can be counted on to do, he rose to the occasion with style and grace. Such tremendous success couldn't happen to a nicer person.

It didn't take a genius to predict that Michael was going to win most of the awards for which he had been nominated—and he had been nominated for more than anyone else in the history of the Grammy. At the very beginning of the telecast, an interviewer went out and buttonholed people on the street to ask them who they thought would win. The answer was unanimously in favor of Michael Jackson; as one fan—a man who looked to be in his fifties—put it, "Michael's just doing so much. He's a thriller!"

But by the time the evening was over, the

scope of Michael's success was greater than even his biggest fans might have dared hope. At the beginning of the program, it was announced that he had already won one award before the show went on the air, for Best Rock Vocal Performance by a Male. In the course of the televised proceedings, Michael Jackson was up for eleven more awards. Only four of those eluded his grasp. He finished the evening with a total of eight awards. As guest presenter Joan Rivers said jokingly, "Tito, please back up the truck!"

One of the nicest things about the evening was that Michael himself seemed truly excited and happy about his good fortune. He arrived looking composed and in good spirits. He was dressed in the military uniform style that has recently been his favorite. This particular costume was a knockout. Over a pair of black sequined pants, he wore a black sequined jacket cut with wide lapels and falling to just below the waist. It was double-breasted, and fastened with huge gold buttons. On each shoulder was a mammoth epaulette. Slung across his chest was a mock bandolier, also in gold. Underneath the jacket he wore a white wing-collared dress shirt, but without the white tie. To complete the outfit, he wore his trademark spangled glove on one hand, and also a spangled wrist band. And, perhaps to camouflage his shyness, he hid his eyes behind dark aviator sunglasses.

At Michael's side was Brooke Shields, who has been his date for several public functions. She looked radiant in white, and could be seen throughout the evening clapping enthusiastically every time Michael got an award. And Michael also brought another guest: the diminutive Emmanuel Lewis, the child star of the TV series *Webster*. He seemed just as excited over Michael's success as Brooke did; all told, they made a very winsome and youthful trio.

The first award for which Michael Jackson was nominated was one he didn't win — for Best Song of the Year with "Billie Jean". He was edged out by the Police with "Every Breath You Take." Shortly thereafter, he made his first trip to the podium, when he and Quincy Jones were selected Producers of the Year for the *Thriller* album. When Michael's name was announced as the winner, the audience rose to its feet for the first of what was to be a series of standing ovations. Quincy spoke first, thanking a long list of people who helped with the album. He concluded by especially thanking "Michael Jackson and his beautiful family," and calling Michael "one of the greatest entertainers in the twentieth century." That brought a cascade of screams from the fans who had managed to nab the coveted balcony seats, and the volume of their screams escalated as Michael stepped to the microphone. But he contented himself with a simple one-liner: "Thank you and I love you all."

Like any good entertainer, Michael knows how to build his evening's act. The next time he was back on the podium, this time to accept the award for Album of the Year, he stayed a little longer. After expressing his thanks for the great honor, he diplomatically went on to thank his recording label, Epic records, calling it "the best record company in the world". He even asked its president, Walter Yetnikoff, to come up on stage with him. Michael also thanked Quincy Jones, "one of my best friends in the world and the best producer" and then, somewhat more seriously, went on to mention the industry's debt to entertainers of an earlier day, mentioning in particular the name of Jackie Wilson. As he concluded his affectionate remarks, the fans in the balcony began to shriek, "I love you" at him.

A little bit later, it was announced that Michael had won two more awards. He was awarded a Grammy as Best Male Rhythm-and-Blues Vocal for his performance on "Billie Jean"; as songwriter, he also got the credit for the Best New Rhythm-and-Blues-Song for that same tune. At that point, he had won five Grammys and you could see that he was really beginning to enjoy himself. He laughed at the presenters' jokes (such as they were) and clapped his hands and waved his arms in time to the gospel singing of Albertina Washington. He especially seemed to enjoy the appearance of Chuck Berry, who was receiving a special award for his lifetime contribution to music. As Chuck did his patented duckwalk across the stage, Michael grinned and cheered.

As television audiences watched the parade of stars presenting and receiving awards, they were also anxiously awaiting the commercial breaks. And, for a change, not so they could rush to the kitchen to whip up a giant sandwich. No, they were waiting to *see* a commercial—the Pepsi Cola commercial starring Michael Jackson (and the other Jacksons too) the filming of which so nearly resulted in a tragic accident when Michael's hair caught on fire.

Even without the news of the near-disaster, the Pepsi commercial would have been headline stuff. Signing the Jacksons to do a commercial—actually, they signed to do two of them—was a real coup for the soft-drink manufacturer, and is expected to be a powerful weapon in its battle with Coca-Cola for the hearts and minds of cola drinkers everywhere. The Jacksons' fee for making the two sixty-second spots was $5,500,000 (that comes out to nearly $50,000 per second, a comfortable rate of pay.) But Pepsi didn't hesitate. They figured that an association with Michael Jackson would be a priceless asset, especially in attracting the younger people who are such an important part of the soft-drink market. They and their advertising agency, BBD&O, immediately set to work devising a whole new campaign. Focused around the slogan "A New Generation", it would use the two Jacksons' commercials as the centerpiece of a carefully programmed appeal to youth.

The first of the two commercials was shot without incident. It shows the Jacksons walking down the streets of some nameless inner city. As they stroll casually along, the camera cuts to another group—younger kids, much like the Jacksons when they first burst on the scene. The ringleader of this group is a cocky kid who, in his look and his walk, is strongly reminiscent of the young Michael Jackson. The climax of the commercial comes when the young Michael-imitator backs into the real Michael Jackson; the boy turns and does a funny doubletake. Michael, of course, is cool. He smiles and waves at the kid as the Jacksons stroll slowly on their way. It's a good commercial, with its little bit of plotline and its teasing visual clues to the action that the viewer must unravel.

With the first commercial safely in the can, Pepsi went on to shoot the second one, the one that pulled out all the stops. (It was about this time that the president of Pepsi Cola, a man in the prime of his life, asked rather plaintively, "Who's this Michael Jackson that all the fuss is about?") It was to be a big production number, budgeted at about one million dollars (not counting the Jacksons fee, of course.) Bob Giraldi was hired to direct, and they decided to set the commercial inside the Shrine Auditorium in Los Angeles—ironically, the very same place where the Grammy Award ceremonies would later be held.

The theme of the commercial was to be the Jacksons in concert. On the first day of shooting, the crew worked with just the Jacksons and shot some of the little backstage details: Michael's glove, his feet in spangled socks doing a little dance step, Tito swigging down a cold Pepsi, moments in the dressing room. On the second day, they were scheduled to shoot the mock concert. Giraldi had handed out tickets to 400 kids who eagerly filled the auditorium; he also hired 100 actors and placed them strategically, just in case the crowd didn't work up the necessary enthusiasm.

On the morning of the shoot, there was a bad omen. Michael went to the men's room and was soon heard calling out in distress. Somehow, his trademark spangled glove had fallen into the toilet bowl; Pepsi executives rushed to the rescue. The glove was fished out, washed carefully, blown dry with a hair dryer, and returned to Michael. The show could go on.

The script called for the rest of the Jacksons to be playing on stage. Michael would descend a set of stairs, emerging from a cloud of colored smoke to join his brothers. The cameras would shoot lots of footage of the crowd reacting to the Jacksons, and of course it would also shoot the Jacksons doing various bits of stage business. Michael's entrance was a critical point in the commercial—really its climax. They tried the shot several times, and it seemed like the smoke cloud was just not thick enough. It was decided to use a little more of the flash powder and some merlin comets to provide flashes of light. During the last take, Michael's pomaded hair caught on fire, perhaps from a spark or maybe just from the heat of the special effects.

When it happened, there was a brief period of pandemonium. Michael began to scream, and his quick-thinking bodyguard Miko (Marlon Brando's son) wrestled him to the ground and put the fire out with his hands and a jacket. Someone filled a T-shirt with ice to make a compress, and a few minutes later, Michael was taken to the emergency room at Cedars-Sinai Medical Center. Upon examination, the medical staff discovered an area, about the size of an orange, of second-degree burns on the back of his head. In the very center was a spot, the size of a flashlight battery, of more serious third-degree burns. He was treated with an application of antiseptic cream and a mild pain-killer. Later, his own doctor, plastic surgeon Dr. Steven Hoefflin (the surgeon who was responsible for the reshaping of Michael's nose), came to see him, and to reassure him. Just to be on the safe side, Dr. Hoefflin decided to transfer Michael to the Burn Center at Brotman Medical Center in Culver City.

As it turned out, Michael's stay was a short one—just 18 hours. As his doctor predicted, "Michael is healthy and in good shape. That will make for a speedy recovery." For a few days after his discharge, he continued to wear a small bandage over the burned area (camouflaged by a hat). But he was fully recovered in time to attend a party thrown in his honor by CBS the week after the accident.

Meanwhile, the Pepsi Cola people worried about what to do next. They had a lot of money tied up in that commercial, and they wanted to use it if it was feasible. On the other hand, it wouldn't do their image any good if people who viewed the commercial associated it with the fact that it nearly killed Michael Jackson. Executives assessed the reaction daily, and finally decided that there was no real feeling of blame towards Pepsi in connection with the accident. They decided to go ahead.

In assembling the final cut, they had to do without the footage in that final take; it had been confiscated by lawyers for both Michael Jackson and Pepsi Cola, in case there might be grounds for a negligence suit. (To date, no such action has been taken.) But Bob Giraldi had shot six and a half miles of film, so there was plenty to work with. And as the commercial went through its final edit, Michael Jackson himself began to take an interest in the process. Michael's contract guaranteed that he would not be shown either holding or drinking Pepsi; he felt that might compromise his artistic integrity. And earlier, he had turned down the song written for the commercial in favor of adapting his song "Billie Jean" with new lyrics. Now he began to press the film editors to remove several shots of him from the finished commercial. For obvious reasons, Pepsi didn't want to make Michael unhappy, so they agreed to his requests. In the final cut, there is only one brief (three-second) closeup of Michael.

But the Pepsi Cola people had no reason to be unhappy with the result. Interest in the commercial was phenomenal. MTV offered to show the clip without advertising charges, as part of their regular programming. *Rolling Stone* called to say they'd like to publish Michael's new lyrics to the melody of "Billie Jean". Television stations all over the country showed brief clips of the commercial on their news broadcasts the night before the Grammy Awards, and announced that its first showing would come on that program. By the time the commercial was actually aired that night, it had an eager audience of millions. The huge budget and the nervous strain notwithstanding, Pepsi seems to have made an excellent investment.

Once the excitement of the commercial had abated, it was time to get back to the serious business. How many more awards would Michael win?

His next, the sixth of the evening, was for the ill-fated album *E.T. The Extraterrestrial,* which won for Best Children's Album. Michael seemed ecstatic; it was clear proof of how much working on that project had really meant to him. He bubbled, "Children are a great inspiration, but this album is not just for children, it's for everyone. I thank everyone, and I'm just so happy." Quincy Jones, who picked up the producer's share of the award, was not quite so happy. He said bluntly, "I *don't* thank the people who kept the record from coming out"—a reference to the lawsuit that stopped the record's distribution.

Next there was a brief round of applause of Bruce Swedien, who won a Grammy for his engineering work on *Thriller.* Things were starting to get exciting, with the big awards of the evening coming into sight. The first to be announced was Best Pop Male Vocalist—and once again, Michael was the winner. By this time, he had made so many trips to the podium that his shyness was beginning to wear off. And the audience began to get a glimpse of the warm and affectionate human being behind the legend. Michael's first remark when he got up on stage was, "When something like this happens to you, you want those who are very dear to you to be with you." Then he asked his sisters to come up with him; soon LaToya, Janet and Maureen were at his side, and you could see how happy he was to share the moment. His first thanks went to God, and then he thanked his father and mother. They were sitting side by side in the auditorium, looking just as proud as you would expect them to. Michael joked, "My mother's very shy, she's like me, she won't come up." But you could see the smile in her eyes as she looked at her young genius, the only one of her sons still living at home with her. Joe Jackson, whose own interest in music and performing started the whole thing, looked fulfilled, and happy to be sharing this moment with the family. Michael completed the circle a moment later, when he said he wanted to thank all his brothers, adding pointedly, "whom I love dearly . . . including Jermaine." Rumors of rifts within the Jackson family were suddenly impossible to believe.

Then Michael indulged in a wonderful piece of showmanship. Throughout the evening, he had taken refuge behind the darkness of his glasses, allowing us to see only his smile. Now he told us, "I made a deal with myself. If I won one more award, I would take off my glasses." He looked anxiously out at the crowd. "I don't want to take them off . . ." The fans began yelling vociferously, and even the stars and communications execs began to clap supportively. Michael went on, "Katharine Hepburn, who's a dear friend of mine, told me I should do it." He reached nervously for the glasses, lowered his hand again. By this time, the tension had built to a fever pitch. "So I'm doing it for her," concluded Michael, "and for the girls in the balcony." Slowly, he reached for the glasses and finally they came off—revealing a composed star, smiling at his audience. There are performers who can get up on the stage and take off all their clothes with less effect than Michael got from the simple act of removing those sunglasses. It was the climax of the entire evening.

The next event was the presentation of the award for Best Female Pop Vocalist to a surprised and nearly tearful Irene Kara, and then came the highlight of the entire evening: the Grammy for Record of the Year. Michael, one of the nominees, had not returned to his seat after his last award, but instead stood backstage, next to Irene, who was another of the nominees. When Michael's name was read, he kissed Irene then bounded out onto the stage. Finally, the happy child in him was showing through. He and Quincy hugged each other repeatedly, and then Michael and Quincy both started to jump up and down. It was a happy and touching moment.

Michael Jackson had just won more Grammy

awards than anyone else in history—another statistic that now belongs to him. (The previous record-holder was Paul Simon, who took home seven awards in 1970.) His awards acknowledged the various aspects of his musical genius. He had been recognized as a songwriter, as a record producer, as a narrator of children's records, and as a vocalist in the fields of rock, rhythm-and-blues, and pop. He had been greeted by standing ovations every time he walked up to the podium. Walter Yetnikoff said he had "shown us the way in music and in song and in dance . . . and as a man." Quincy Jones repeatedly hailed Michael's genius. His family was all there, cheering him on, making him feel their pride. His date and his friend were applauding loudly. The moment was entirely Michael Jackson's.

But his reaction to this moment that was the capstone to his achievement was a characteristically generous one. First, he gave his thanks to the public, saying "I love you all," and then mischievously adding, "I love all the girls in the balcony." This created such pandemonium that he had to wait some time before he could be heard over the happy screams.

And it turned out that what he wanted to say next was to pay tribute to a colleague, Lionel Ritchie. Lionel had been nominated for a large number of Grammys himself, for his singing, songwriting, and producing on his album,

All Night Long. It's a good album, and Ritchie is a talented musician with devoted fans of his own. It was just his misfortune to release his album in the same year that Michael Jackson released *Thriller.* Every category in which Lionel was nominated put him in head-to-head competition with Michael, and in every case Michael won. It must have been a very disappointing night for Lionel. He behaved like a gentleman, but he must have been deeply chagrined to find himself totally shut out of the awards. He probably felt he was the butt of the joke Joan Rivers cracked when she explained why she was going to read the rules of the awards: "Every one of the nominees out there should know exactly why they lost out to Michael Jackson."

But with his usual kindness and thoughtfulness, Michael was aware of Lionel's feelings. He made a point of praising Lionel as "a wonderful person and a wonderful songwriter." He went on the intimate that Lionel had been one of his heroes since he was ten years old. Lionel recoiled in mock-horror at being thus relegated to an older generation. The exchange ended with easy and warm laughter. While it probably didn't send Lionel Ritchie home exactly happy, at least it gave him a little bit of his due.

And it gave audiences one more clue to the reason that Michael Jackson is so greatly admired, so devotedly loved. Throughout the entire evening, he had shown enormous consideration for the feelings of others — a character trait not normally associated with superstars of any kind. He took the trouble to praise Quincy Jones and thank him for all his help. He spoke warmly of his record company and its president, probably a rare occurrence for Walter Yetnikoff, since most recording stars are quick to blame their record label and slow to give it credit. Michael openly displayed his love and gratitude for his family, and went out of his way to include Jermaine, slightly distanced from the rest of the family since the time of the Motown departure, and his father, who also had reason to feel slightly isolated. Perhaps most endearing of all was the fact that he clearly recognized that those noisy "girls in the balcony" — the ones who interrupted him with screams and shouts, and who would certainly mob him if they got the chance — should also be thanked, for the loyalty and devotion and eagerness to buy his album that has put Michael Jackson on top. Michael Jackson may be shy, and he may be afraid of those girls and their power to harm him because of their sheer numbers. But he still cherishes his emotional connection with the girls in the balcony . . . and all the rest of us who love him.

MICHAEL JACKSON TODAY . . . AND TOMORROW

Today Michael Jackson stands at the pinnacle of his profession. *Thriller* has just made it into the *Guinness Book of World Records* as the all-time best-selling solo record album, with sales reaching nearly 25,000,000 copies worldwide. It is still Number One on the album charts, and it continues to sell at the rate of nearly 60,000 copies a day. That's a stupendous achievement, which may never be equalled by another artist.

But for Michael Jackson, it comes simply as one more milestone in the career of a young man who has broken records all his life. He is certainly one of the youngest performers ever to establish himself as a major recording artist. He's had an amazing number of hit singles, starting with "I Want You Back" in 1969. There are now 12 in all, with and without his brothers, that have made it all the way to the Number One spot. He's a sell-out concert attraction as the lead singer of The Jacksons. He's a major winner of awards in the music business, winning his first in 1971 for Best Male Vocalist, and his most recent in 1984, a total of 8 Grammies.

All these rewards and successes reflect his widespread personal popularity. Because of the enormous public response to his personality, there is virtually a Michael Jackson Communications Industry, providing employment for scores of people: makers of calendars and posters, publishers of music magazines, vendors of buttons and memorabilia (and of course, writers of books). His picture on the cover sells magazines automatically, and feature stories about Michael Jackson fill even news broadcasts on television.

I discovered for myself that the range of people who love and admire Michael Jackson is truly amazing. For example . . . when I began working on this book, I talked to a friend who is herself a singer, appearing in restaurants and small clubs in New York, doing a bit of recording, trying to sell some songs she'd written: in other words, a seasoned pro in the disillusioning music biz. But when she spoke about Michael Jackson, she was just as starry-eyed and breathless as any teenage girl, raving on and on about his voice, his looks, his dancing. A few days later, I discussed the book with a black recording artist who's been turning out albums and appearing live for nearly two decades. He too spoke of Michael Jackson, twenty years his junior, with awe and reverence, freely labeling him a genius, saying repeatedly, "I *respect* the guy." Then my cleaning lady spotted the pictures of Michael on my desk—and it turned out that she loved every one of his hits. She had followed his career since his boyhood years with the Jackson Five, and she expressed warm motherly concern about how hard it must be to live in the limelight for so many years (she thinks he ought to get married, so he won't be so lonely.) A therapist friend called almost daily to ask for bulletins on new facts my research had uncovered. But another friend, a writer herself, announced she was going to stop calling me at all, because hearing about the Michael Jackson project made her so jealous she couldn't stand it.

The breadth of Michael Jackson's appeal, and the fact that so many people feel so strongly devoted to him, is unprecedented. Most performers could not hope to equal either Michael's achievements or his appeal, even in a lifetime of effort. But he is just 25 years old. Artistically, he is still maturing . . . and still ambitious. It is almost impossible to predict the heights that he might achieve in the future.

For Michael Jackson is still developing his full potential. Not just as an artist, but also as a popular idol. In fact, Michael Jackson the artist is currently in the process of creating Michael Jackson the legend, the public persona, the icon for the Eighties. The image of Michael Jackson, which he is so carefully composing, is one that reflects and also shapes the culture of our times.

Marshall Berman, professor of political science at the City University of New York, explains why: "The time is right for Michael Jackson, because American culture has gotten better at handling sex and playing with gender roles. He gives you the sense that you can play with anything — with being man or woman, black or white, scared or scary, or some funny combination of all of them."

Michael's image is frequently labeled "androgynous" and compared with that of Mick Jagger or David Bowie. But this comparison is to some extent misleading. Bowie and Jagger have in the past exhibited on-stage images that *blur* the distinctions between the sexes. Prince does the same thing today, with his makeup and his high heels . . . and his tough-guy lyrics. The intention of these performers is to puzzle you about their sex, to resist being put in one category or the other, to reject traditionally assigned gender roles.

Michael Jackson is different. His genius is that he celebrates — and encompasses — both sexes. He's not so much androgynous as he is what might be called "bipolar."

The two best-selling posters of Michael illustrate this bipolarity very neatly. Go into any shop that sells posters and you will see them there, side by side. In one, Michael is wearing the tough-guy cliché of a dark leather jacket with a big collar, a plain T-shirt, an old faded pair of jeans. He is standing in a typically masculine pose: legs spread apart, hips cocked in a way that thrusts his groin forward. Even the position of his hands is classic male beefcake: one is inside his pocket, the other loosely hooked over pocket's edge with a casually pointing forefinger; both hands are sight-lined toward his crotch. The other poster creates an image that is the exact opposite. It shows Michael in a soft pastel sweater; on his breast there is a huge jewel with suggestively dangling pendants. His hair is soft, and a few curls escape down the back of his collar and over his forehead. In the most frequently seen version of this poster, Michael is cut off just below the waist, a photographic neutering of his image. In an alternate version, you can see only that he is wearing very loose white flannel trousers with big front pleats, a style that totally camouflages the crotch; and his folded hands are totally hidden in capacious pockets.

The two posters really form a complete set, and to understand Michael Jackson's image, you have to pay equal attention to both of them. He is no Boy George, dressing himself up in women's clothes and presenting a kind of travesty of the sex (and one, moreover, that is offensive to women since it is based on the assumption that femininity consists merely of clothes and makeup.) When Michael emphasizes the feminine side of his nature, he does so not by transvestitism but by focusing on qualities that are traditionally considered feminine, such as delicacy, sensitivity, the love of beauty, emotional responsiveness. Then he dresses accordingly. His recent plastic surgery, which narrowed and refined his nose and widened his eyes, also helps him achieve the look.

Yet his expression of these feminine qualities doesn't bar him from an equal and opposite display of the best of the qualities generally considered masculine: athletic superiority, high-energy physical presence, daring action in a crisis (the theme of the "Beat It" video). The sum of these two halves of the Michael Jackson persona is a complete portrait of humanity.

Another significant aspect of the Michael Jackson image, and its widespread appeal, is the ability to combine the virtues of both maturity and childishness. As a professional entertainer, Michael is well-known to be disciplined, hard-working, responsible, and reliable. He doesn't miss or cancel performances; he stays in the recording studio as long as necessary to do a good job; he never shirks his share of either the work or the responsibility. But the other side of his public personality emphasizes his childishness. He lives at home with his mother; he wants to have Disneyworld inside his very own house; he keeps a menagerie of birds and exotic pets, such as a llama and a boa constrictor; he avoids the emotional commitments of real romantic love, marriage, and parenthood. When he must go out into the adult world socially, as for instance when his attendance at a party is required, he wears a costume, like a child playing dress-up.

To his fans, Michael Jackson seems to portray the best of both worlds. He illustrates adult virtues in the context of the lifestyle of a child. Thus he avoids the criticism that is typically leveled at the entertainer with a totally childlike attitude toward everything, even his work, at the same time that he appears to avoid the boredom and constriction that are sometimes associated with the "serious" world of the adult.

In today's culture, this combination speaks to many people's desires. For several decades, our society has been conspicuously youth-oriented, as we all try to look and dress like we are in our twenties — and maintain the same level of physical fitness. But there has been increasing criticism of the selfishness and immaturity of this attitude. Now Michael Jackson shows us how to surmount it. Professionally, we behave like the most responsible of adults; personally, we sustain ourselves in a fantasy world of youth.

And Michael's particular brand of youthful fantasy even counters the objections that such behavior is self-centered or emotionally stunted. Yes, it's true that he has so far evaded the adult responsibilities that go along with a total commitment to some other person, but he has never behaved irresponsibly toward anyone either. And to compensate for the fact that he hasn't fallen in love with any individual, he has become a personification of the spirit of love. He has in fact achieved, in his own way, the spiritual condition that eastern philosophers endorse as the highest plane to which the human spirit can aspire. He has replaced the love for a particular person with a generalized love for all people.

It is within this context of his general warmth and kindliness toward all humanity that the question of Michael Jackson's color can best be interpreted. For surely one aspect of his enormous success that is singularly impressive is the fact that he has achieved it as a black artist in a predominately white culture. When Michael began his career twenty years ago, he started from within the black community, with talent contests in Harlem and nightclub appearances on the chitling circuit. Perhaps Michael's youth and innocence were part of the reason he was initially accepted outside that community by the larger white culture. They were certainly the reason he was able to get up in front of white audiences and sing songs with sexually bold lyrics while he pranced and strutted across the stage. The same performance from a sexually mature and aggressive black man would be likely to make those audiences uncomfortable.

But of course, Michael did eventually become a sexually mature male. Yet his performances were still accepted by the white cultural mainstream. Tom Carson, writing in the *Village Voice*, has suggested that one reason is the undeniable fact that Michael's sexuality is never directed *at* anyone. Although certainly powerful, his sexuality is diffuse, generalized. In other words, it is again aimed at all humanity rather than at any one specific listener—and that makes it acceptable.

By the same token, it makes Michael's blackness acceptable too. No one has ever accused Michael Jackson of being an Oreo, black on the outside and white on the inside. He has remained exceptionally faithful to the black musical tradition in which his career was rooted, and even his family life seems to fall squarely within an identifiable black cultural tradition. But although he seems perfectly comfortable with his black heritage, he never lets himself be limited by it, or by the responses—his own or other people's—of a traditional attitude. Michael Jackson says color is unimportant to him, and his actions confirm the truth of the statement. It's just one more way in which he prefers to focus not on the specific individual, but on the whole of humanity; not on the specifics of one man's skin but on the generalities of the human condition.

His attitude makes it hard for his audiences to do anything other than emulate his lofty principles. The result is a black performer, working within a black musical tradition, who is able to fuse that with elements from the white musical repertoire and become widely and easily accepted by the white mainstream culture.

One question that is frequently raised by Michael's devoted fans, and also by some of the people who are closest to him personally, is how difficult it must be for him to exist as the ever-so-public personality called Michael Jackson. What is the emotional cost of his fame? How hard is it to keep his balance in the glare of the spotlight? What happens to the human being who stands behind the public image?

On the one hand, you have to give Michael Jackson credit for being a fundamentally tough character, a psychological survivor. He has stood in the limelight for most of his life, and he shows himself still totally capable of sustaining the pressure of that position with poise and grace. He doesn't disappoint his fans, he shows no signs of a superstar's temperament. He has remained a thoroughly nice and kind person.

He is particularly appealing because of the way he likes to do things for other people. For example, a charming story turned up recently in *Rock*, written by a young woman who encountered Michael roaming around a country inn in California. He was obviously shy but perfectly delightful: he showed her how to adjust her new camera, posed for pictures with his arm around her, and gave her his private number so she could call to let him know how the photos turned out. Another instance of his unspoiled sweetness emerged at the time of his accident on the set of a Pepsi-Cola commercial, when the back of his head was burned. Not only did he go to see other patients in the burn ward of the hospital (a location even medical professionals consider the most draining place in the world) but it turned out that he had been stopping by to visit some of the critically ill patients all along . . . without fanfare or promotion.

But Michael's friends and family do observe that he has paid—and continues to pay—a price for what he gives the public. Jane Fonda told a reporter, "In some ways, Michael reminds me of the walking wounded. He's an extremely fragile person. I think that just getting on with life, making contact with people, is hard enough, much less to be worried about whither goest the world." Diana Ross, to whom Michael says he confides many of his deepest feelings, worries too. "He spends a lot of time, too much time, by himself. I try to get him out. I rented a boat and took my children and Michael on a cruise. Michael has a lot of people around him, but he's very afraid. I don't know why. I think it came from the early days." And his mother worries about the effects of the constant pursuit by love-crazed fans. "There are so many," she says wearily. "You have no idea what's really going on in their minds. That's why it's going to be so hard for my son to get a wife."

Michael himself expresses an ambivalent attitude toward the demands of his position. On the one hand, he has said that he considers the stage his real home, "the place where I'm supposed to be, where God meant me to be." In fact, he claims that only on the stage does he really feel free. On the other hand, being on stage means being surrounded by those crowds of fans, and that's difficult, threatening." He told *Rolling Stone*'s Gerri Hirshey what it was like: "Girls in the lobby, coming up the stairway. You hear guards getting them out of elevators. But you stay in your room and write a song. And when you get tired of that, you talk to yourself. Then let it all out onstage."

Michael made the contrast between his public existence and his private self even clearer in another interview, this time with a *Newsweek* reporter. "My whole life has been onstage. And the impression I get of people is applause, standing ovations and running after you. In a crowd, I'm afraid. Onstage, I feel safe. If I could, I would sleep on the stage. I'm serious."

Michael admits that he is painfully shy when it comes to being with people one-on-one. He said, "My brothers say that *everybody* intimidates me. That's not true, but I do avoid eye contact with a lot of people." He added, "I'd much rather talk on the phone," and then made a touching confession: "I'm much deeper in conversation on the phone than I am in person."

The picture that emerge from all these clues is of a person who is holding the world at bay. He prefers to talk to even his best friends over the phone rather than in person. And he says that when he does see friends, like Liza Minnelli, the conversation is all performance-oriented: exchanging anecdotes, tips, dance steps . . . in other words, show biz shoptalk. Brooke Shields says she likes him because he is a consummate professional. It all seems a little sad, a little empty.

It seems likely that when Michael Jackson is not performing for an audience, he feels deeply alone — except for the family that has always been there for him, with whom he always feels comfortable. And of course, for him, there is also the sustaining presence of God. Michael is a strongly religious person, who adheres faithfully to the tenets of his religion. He believes in God and he believes in the power of prayer: "I get down on my knees every night and thank God and ask him to lead the way."

And in his own way, Michael has learned some mechanisms for coping with the distance he feels from ordinary life, the fear he sometimes feels when confronted with ordinary people. One of these coping mechanisms is to wear a single white glove. He wears it all the time now. Even at the time of his recent burning accident, he insisted to the ambulance attendants that he wanted to keep his spangled glove on when they wheeled him into the hospital emergency room. The glove has become such a trademark that when CBS threw a big party for Michael Jackson right after he came out of the hospital, each invitation included one white glove for the party-goer, to wear to honor Michael—and to prove at the door the genuine status of invited guest.

It doesn't take a psychiatrist to come up with some theories about the significance of that white glove. It is a symbol of his own spiritual purity and also a protection against the dirt and corruption of the outside world. But it's interesting to hear what Michael himself says about the meaning of the glove. To him, it signifies his role as an entertainer. It is a costume, a disguise, a way to communicate the fact that he is "on", rather than simply being a private person. And so long as he can see himself in the role of entertainer, he can deal with the world very successfully.

So Michael Jackson is a man who has learned to live in the terrible and constant glare of the limelight and at the same time protect his vulnerable creativity. Some of his coping mechanisms may be a bit unusual, and the balance he has reached may be a delicate one. But he is able to work well, to love his family, to nourish his creativity, to maintain his spiritual values. And although there may be a lot of gossip about Michael Jackson—about his supposed homosexuality, his odd reclusiveness, the rumour that he'd gotten some girl pregnant, the speculation about hormone treatments to keep his voice high, and so on and on—it is surely indicative that not even the most scurrilous gossip ever mentions Michael Jackson ever hurting anyone.

The cliché says that to get to the top, you must trample on people along the way. But no one has ever come forward to claim the status of victim of Michael Jackson's trampling. All the people who have worked with him have nothing but good to say about him. He seems to have treated them well, paid them generously, seen to it that they got full credit for their work, and done all he could to see that their careers benefitted from their association with him. There are very few other human beings, in show business or outside of it, who have such a good record in regard to their personal dealings with their business associates.

What does the future hold for Michael Jackson? Certainly more work. There's that new album, and the scheduled collaborations with other artists as well. There are plans for a movie with Steven Spielberg. And a new creative outlet opened up in Michael's life when Doubleday paid him a $300,000 advance for his autobiography, and they announced at the same time that his editor would be none other than Jacqueline Onassis. He met her through her children John and Caroline, who are both Michael Jackson fans, and she encouraged him to think seriously about a book project. In addition to containing several hundred rare photographs from his personal collection, the book will focus on his professional life. He will write about the way he works out his dance routines, about his techniques of singing, performing and songwriting. It ought to be a very interesting book, and publishing people are already predicting it will reach the best-seller list.

What the future holds for Michael Jackson personally is somewhat harder to predict. He says he would like to get married, have children. (Can you imagine what it would be like to grow up with Michael Jackson for a father? A real fantasy childhood) On the other hand, he also says that he's not ready for any such step just yet. He will soon move back into the Encino house he has just remodeled, to live with his mother and his sisters LaToya and Janet. He will continue to see his brothers, and his nieces and nephews—he loves the company of children; feels at his most free and relaxed when he is around them.

His father, recently divorced from his mother, appears to be on the fringe of Michael Jackson's life these days. Even their professional connection has been severed. In the summer of 1983, it was announced that Joe Jackson, and the firm of Wiesner/DeMann Entertainment, would no longer represent Michael Jackson. Ron Wiesner and Freddy DeMann said the problem was principally with Joe Jackson, no longer in the confidence either of his son Michael or of the executives at Epic Records. Joe Jackson, in a public statement, seemed to blame the rift on mysterious advisors who urged Michael into a professional breakup with his family. In any case it was sports promoter Don King who emerged as the power behind the Jacksons' 1984 summer tour.

But the Jackson family continues to provide Michael with most of his emotional support. And then there are his friends . . . all those famous and successful people whose attitudes toward Michael are a compound of admiration and protectiveness. Recently, he told a reporter that he had made some friends who are "civilians" — people outside show business, people who might help him relax more fully.

The first line of Michael Jackson's favorite book, *Peter Pan*, reads, "All children, except one, grow up." For nearly a decade, through a combination of intense will power and dedicated focus, Michael has tried to emulate that child . . . with results that have obviously been helpful to his creative development. But even Peter Pan eventually found that perpetual childhood was a sad situation, and there are certainly signs that Michael too feels the strain. With his intelligence and his great emotional honesty, he is not the man to allow himself to be trapped in a false position. Sooner or later, Michael Jackson is going to enter fully into the adult world, with its increased commitments, its acceptance of painful limitations. For a talent as great as Michael's, the chances are good that such a step forward will serve to increase the power of his artistic expression—and therefore all of us Michael Jackson fans have a lot to look forward to.

DISCOGRAPHY

1969

Diana Ross Presents the Jackson Five
Released by Motown
Produced by Bobby Taylor and The Corporation

"My Cherie Amour"
"Who's Lovin' You"
"Chained"
"I Know I'm Losing You"
"Stand"
"Born to Love You"

"Zip A Dee Doo Dah"
"Nobody"
"I Want You Back"
"Can You Remember"
"Standing In the Shadows of Love"
"You've Changed"

1970

ABC
Released by Motown
Produced by Hal Davis and The Corporation

"ABC"
"The Love You Save"
"La La"
"I Found That Girl"
"I Bet You"
"Don't Know Why I Love You"
"The Young Folks"
"Never Had a Dream Come True""

Third Album
Released by Motown
Produced by The Corporation

"I'll Be There""
"Mama's Pearl"

"Oh How Happy"
"Bridge Over Troubled Waters"
"The Love I Saw In You Was Just a Mirage"
"Goin' Back to Indiana"
"Ready or Not"
"Can I See You in the Morning"
"How Funky is Your Chicken"
"Reach In"
"Darling Dear"

The Jackson Five Christmas Album
Released by Motown
Produced by Hal Davis and The Corportion

"I Saw Mommy Kissing Santa Claus"
"Christmas Won't Be the Same Again"
"Santa Claus is Coming to Town"
"The Christmas Song"
"Up on the Housetop"
"Frosty the Snowman"
"The Little Drummer Boy"
"Rudolph the Red-Nosed Reindeer"
"Give Love on Christmas Day"
"Someday at Christmas"

1971

Maybe Tomorrow
Released by Motown
Produced by The Corporation

"Never Can Say Goodbye"
"Maybe Tomorrow"
"Sixteen Candles"
"Honey Chile"
"The Wall"
"Petals"
"It's Great to Be Here"

Goin' Back to Indiana
Released by Motown
Soundtrack of the Jackson Five television special.

"Goin' Back to Indiana""
"Stand"
"I Want to Take You Higher"
"Feelin' Alright"

The Jackson Five's Greatest Hits
Released by Motown
Produced by The Corporation

"Sugar Daddy"
"I Want You Back"
"Maybe Tomorrow"
"Goin' Back to Indiana"
"ABC"
"Mama's Pearl"
"Who's Loving You"
"I'll Be There"
"Never Can Say Goodbye"

1972

Got To Be There (solo)
Released by Motown
Produced by The Corporation and Hal Davis
Executive Producer: Berry Gordy

"Ain't No Sunshine"
"I Wanna Be Where You Are"
"Girl Don't Take You Love From Me"
"In Our Small Way"
"Got To Be There"
"Rockin' Robin"

"Wings of My Love"
"Maria"
"Love is Here and Now You're Gone"
"You've Got a Friend"

Looking Through the Windows
Released by Motown
Produced by Hal Davis, Jonny Bristol, Willie Hutch, Jerry Marcellino, Mel Larson.
Executive Producer: Berry Gordy

"Ain't Nothing Like the Real Thing"
"Lookin' Through the Windows"
"Don't Let Your Baby Catch You"
"To Know"
"Doctor My Eyes"
"E-Ne-Me-Ne-Mi-Ne-Moe"
"If I Have To Move A Mountain"
"Don't Want To See Tomorrow"
"Children of the Light"
"I Can Only Give You Love"

Ben (solo)
Released by Motown
Produced by The Corporation and Hal Davis

"Ben"
"What Goes Around Comes Around"
"My Girl"

"People Make the World Go Round"
"We've Got A Good Thing Going"
"In Our Small Way"
"Shoo Be Doo Be Doo Da Day"

1973

Skywriter
Released by Motown
Produced by The Corporation

"Corner of the Sky"
"The Boogie Man"
"Hallelujah Day"
"Uppermost"
"I Can't Quit Your Love"
"Touch"
"You Made Me What I Am Today"
"Skywriter"
"World of Sunshine"
"Oh, I'd Love To Be With You"

Music and Me (solo)
Released by Motown
Produced by The Corporation

"Music and Me"
"Johnny Raven"
"Happy"
"Too Young"
"Up Again"
"All The Things You Are"
"Doggin' Around"
"Euphoria"
"Morning Glow"

Get It Together
Released by Motown
Produced by Hal Davis

"Get It Together"
"Don't Say Goodbye Again"
"You Need Love Like I Do"
"Hum Along and Dance"
"Dancing Machine"
"Mama I Gotta Brand New Thing"

1974

Dancing Machine
Released by Motown
Produced by Hal Davis

"Dancing Machine"
"I Am Love"
"Whatever You Got I Want"
"She's a Rhythm Child"
"The Life of the Party"
"What You Don't Know"
"If I Don't Love You This Way"
"It All Begins and Ends with Love"
"The Mirrors of My Mind"

1975

Forever, Michael (solo)
Released by Motown
Produced by Brian Holland, Hal Davis, Sam Brown, and Freddie Perren and Fonce Mizell

"We're Almost There"
"Just a Little Bit of You"
"Take Me Back"
"Dear Michael"
"One Day in Your Life"
"Cinderella Stay Awhile"
"Dapper Dan"
"We've Got Forever"
"You Are There"
"I'll Come Home to You"

Moving Violation
Released by Motown
Produced by Brian Holland, Hal Davis, Jerry Marcellino and Max Larson

"Forever Came Today"
"Moving Violation"
"(You Were Made) Especially For Me"
"Body Language"
"All I Do Is Think of You"
"Honey Love"
"Breezy"
"Call of the Wild"
"Time Explosion"

The Best of Michael Jackson (solo)
Released by Motown
Produced by The Corporation

"Got To Be There"
"Ben"
"With a Child's Heart"
"Happy"
"One Day in Your Life"
"I Wanna Be Where You Are"
"Rockin' Robin"
"We're Almost There"
"Morning Blow"
"Music and Me"

1976

The Jacksons
Released by Epic
Produced by Kenny Gamble and Leon Huff

"Enjoy Yourself"
"Think Happy"
"Good Times"
"Keep on Dancin' "
"Blues Away" (written by Michael Jackson)
"Show You the Way To Go"
"Living Together"
"Strength of One Man"
"Dreamer"
"Style of Life" (written by Michael Jackson and Tito Jackson)

Joyful Jukebox Music
Released by Motown
Produced by Tom Bee, Michael Edward Campbell, Hal Davis, Sam Brown III, Freddie

Perren, Fonce Mizell, Mel Larson and Jerry
Marcellino

"We're Gonna Change Our Style"
"We're Here to Entertain You"
"Joyful Jukebox Music"
"Window Shopping"
"You've My Best Friend, My Love"
"Love is the Thing You Need"
"The Eternal Light"
"Pride and Joy"
"Through Thick and Thin"
"Make Tonight All Mine"

The Jackson Five Anthology
A three record set
Released by Motown
Various Producers

"I Want You Back"
"ABC"
"Don't Know Why I Love You"
"I'll Be There"
"The Love You Save"
"I Found That Girl"
"I Am Love"
"Body Language"
"Forever Came Today"
"Mama's Pearl"
"Got To Be There"

"Goin' Back to Indiana"
"Never Can Say Goodbye"
"Sugar Daddy"
"Maybe Tomorrow"
"Get It Together"
"Dancing Machine"
"Whatever You Got, I Want"
"We're Almost There"
"Just A Little Bit of You"
"All I Do is Think of You"
"Rockin' Robin"
"I Wanna Be Where You Are"
"Ben"
"That's How Love Goes"
"Love Don't Want to Leave"
"Daddy's Home"
"Lookin' Through the Windows"
"Little Bitty Pretty One"
"Corner of the Sky"
"Skywriter"
"Hallelujah Day"
"The Boogie Man"

1977

Goin' Places
Released by Epic
Produced by Kenneth Gamble and Leon Huff

"Music's Taking Over"
"Goin' Places"
"Even Though You're Gone"
"Jump for Joy"
"Heaven Knows I Love You Girl"
"Man of War"
"Do What You Wanna" (by Michael Jackson and Tito Jackson)
"Find Me A Girl"
"Different Kind of Lady" (written by the Jacksons)

1978

Destiny
Released by Epic
Produced by the Jacksons
Executive producers: Bobby Colomby and Mike Atkinson

"Blame It On the Boogie" (written by the Jacksons)
"Push Me Away" (written by the Jacksons)
"Things I Do For You" written by the Jacksons)
"Shake Your Body" (written by Michael Jackson and Randy Jackson)
"Destiny" (written by the Jacksons)

"Bless This Soul" (written by Michael Jackson)
"All Night Dancing" (written by the Jacksons)
"That's What You Get" (written by the Jacksons)

1979

Off the Wall (solo)
Released by Epic
Produced by Quincy Jones

"Don't Stop 'Til You Get Enough" (written and coproduced by Michael Jackson)
"Rock With You"
"Working Day and Night" (written and coproduced by Michael Jackson)
"Get on the Floor" (written by Michael Jackson and Louis Johnson, and coproduced by Michael Jackson)
"Off the Wall"
"Girlfriend"
"She's Out of My Life"
"I Can't Help It"
"It's the Falling in Love"
"Burn This Disco"

1980

Triumph
Released by Epic
Produced by the Jacksons

"Lovely One" (written by the Jacksons)
"Heartbreak Hotel" (written by Michael Jackson)
"Can You Feel It" (written by Michael Jackson and Jackie Jackson)
"Walk Right Now" (written by the Jacksons)
"Your Ways" (written by Jackie Jackson)
"Get Down on the Floor" (written by the Jacksons)
"Time Waits for No One" (written by the Jacksons)
"Wondering Who" (written by the Jacksons)

Boogie
Released by Natural Resources/Motown
Various producers

"Love's Gone Bad"
"I Ain't Gonna Eat My Heart Out Anymore"
"I Was Made To Love Her"
"One Day I'll Marry You"

"Oh, I've Been Blessed"
"Penny Arcade"
"Just Because I Love You"
"ABC"
"Never Can Say Goodbye"
"Dancing Machine"

1981

The Jacksons Live
Released by Epic
Produced by the Jacksons

"Can You Feel It"
"Things I Do For You"
"Off the Wall"
"Ben"
"Heartbreak Hotel"
"She's Out of My Life"
medley of "I Want You Back," "Never Can Say
Goodbye," and "Got To Be There."
"I'll Be There"
"Rock With You"
"Lonely One"
"Working Day and Night"
"Don't Stop 'Til You Get Enough"
"Shake Your Body"

1982

Thriller (solo)
Released by Epic
Produced by Quincy Jones, coproduced by Michael Jackson

"Wanna Be Starting Something" (written by Michael Jackson)
"Baby Be Mine"
"The Girl is Mine" (written by Michael Jackson and Paul McCartney)
"Thriller"
"Beat It" (written by Michael Jackson)
"Billie Jean" (written by Michael Jackson)
"Human Nature""
"P.Y.T. (Pretty Young Thing)"
"The Lady in My Life"

NUMBER ONE SINGLES

I Want You Back (1969)

ABC (1970)
The Love You Save (1970)
I'll Be There (1970)
Mama's Pearl (1971)
Got To Be There (1971) solo
Ben (1972) solo
Don't Stop 'Til You Get Enough (1979) solo
Rock With You (1979) solo
Billie Jean (1983) solo
Beat It (1983) solo

VIDEOS

Blame It On The Boogie (1978) Jacksons
Don't Stop 'Til You Get Enough (1979)
Michael Jackson
Rock With Me (1979) Michael Jackson
The Triumph (1980) Jacksons
Say, Say, Say (1983) Paul McCartney
Billie Jean (1983) Michael Jackson
Beat It (1983) Michael Jackson
Thriller (1983) Michael Jackson

Miscellaneous Recordings

—"Motown At The Hollywood Palace" (Motown, 1970). Live performance.

— "Diana: TV Soundtrack" (Motown, 1971). The soundtrack to Diana Ross's television special.
— "The Motown Story" (Motown, 1970). Michael talks about his life in *The Jackson Five*.
— "Motown Superstars Sing Motown Superstars" (Motown, 1983). Contains the previously unreleased "Ask The Lonely" by *The Jackson Five*
— *Save the Children* (1972). The soundtrack to the documentary.
— *Ben* (1972). The movie. Michael Jackson sings the title song.
— *The Wiz* (1978). The soundtrack from the movie. Michael plays the part of the Scarecrow.
— *E.T.* (1983). The Steven Spielberg record. Michael Jackson narrates the story and wins a Grammy for it.
— "Pipes of Peace" (Columbia, 1983). "The Paul McCartney album. Michael Jackson sings the following duets: "Say, Say, Say" and "The Man."

Solo Albums
by Other Members of the Jackson Family

Jermaine Jackson:
Jermaine (1973)
Come Into My Life (1973)
My Name is Jermaine (1976)
Feel the Fire (1977)
Frontiers (1978)
Jermaine (1980)
Let's Get Serious (1980)
I Like Your Style (1981)
Let Me Tickle Your Fancy (1982)

Jackie Jackson:
Jackie Jackson (1973)

Janet Jackson:
Janet Jackson (1982)

LaToya Jackson:
LaToya Jackson (1980)